Artificial Intelligence
and
National Security

Artificial Intelligence
and
National Security

Prof (Dr) Vijay S Khare

Col Amit Sinha

PENTAGON PRESS LLP

First published in 2024 by
PENTAGON PRESS LLP
206, Peacock Lane, Shahpur Jat
New Delhi-110049, India
Contact: 011-64706243

Typeset in Palatino, 11 Point
Printed by Aegean Offset Printers, Greater Noida

ISBN 978-81-951894-9-6 (HB)

Disclaimer: The views and opinions expressed in the book is the individual assertion of the Authors. The Publisher does not take any responsibility for the same in any manner whatsoever. The same shall solely be the responsibility of the Authors.

www.pentagonpress.in

CONTENTS

FOREWORD

Al has emerged not just as another technological tool but as a paradigm-shifting force that promises to redefine the contours of national security. The digital revolution is a testament to this, with Artificial Intelligence (Al) standing at the forefront. The book, "Artificial Intelligence and National Security," traces its path from inception to its future implications, exploring Al's multifaceted dimensions. It offers a comprehensive insight into its role in shaping the fabric of national security. The exhaustive information reflects the profound depth and breadth of Al and National security, ensuring readers gain a holistic understanding of the subject.

Additionally, the comparative study of the P5 nations sheds light on the global Al landscape, offering invaluable perspectives on our current position and the path forward.

I appreciate the dedication, thoroughness, and vision with which "Artificial Intelligence and National Security" has been crafted.lt serves as an indispensable resource for those involved in policymaking, defense, academia, and those interested in learning about strategic security. May this book disseminate knowledge, ignite curiosity, and foster strategic ideas.

Warm Regards,

Dr G Satheesh Reddy
Distinguished Scientist
Scientific Adviser to Raksha Mantri

PREFACE

The advent of the present millennium has been a witness to major transformations in the form of electronic chips which have significantly revolutionised the current world in a plethora of ways. Carrying forward the notion of the ever-evolving field of technology, the next wave of transformation will be driven by Artificial Intelligence (AI) which is bound to significantly alter the relationship of the hardware and software with human thought processes or 'Wetware', making them intelligent like humans. AI since its inception, has come a long way, evolving from an academic discipline to a game-changing force that has revolutionized numerous sectors, including agriculture, education, healthcare, financial technology, manufacturing, transportation and even military operations. AI and AI-based systems are emerging as vital strategic weapons for National Security in the present modern era, as the ever-changing character of warfare significantly shifts to, what is now referred to as "Fifth Generation Warfare (5GW)".

The aim of publishing this book is to serve as a ready-reckoner on the current status of AI developments globally and help the think-tank of the country in developing a suitable roadmap comprising essential AI-based strategies and contribute towards the National Security of the country.

We have made a genuine attempt in tracing the origins and the resurgence of the technology through the medium of various primary and secondary literary sources which have explored the ideas of credible individuals and have been presented in a simple and lucid manner in order to make the readers understand the vital importance of the technology and its implications in the near future, ultimately providing the readers with a base, building up on which they can develop a clear understanding as to how the technology is going to impact the military operations and hence the National Security in the present era of 5GW.

Delving further into the discussion in developing a suitable roadmap, we have examined the Hybrid Warfare and Grey-Zone Tactics, which our nation has been contending with over the past three decades against Western and Northern adversaries, and have highlighted the utmost importance that 'Algorithmic Warfare' holds in the present times. In order to provide clarity on the same, we have conducted a review of present-day threats, challenges and opportunities related to national security, which highlights the need for a National Security Strategy. This strategy will guide leaders and stakeholders in formulating a roadmap for the implementation of AI strategies, which have become a necessity for national security in the present landscape. In order to support the claims for an AI-based national security roadmap, the proliferation of AI strategies and roadmaps announced by major economies across the globe, especially the P5 nations, has been studied in depth in order to suggest the Indian leaders and think-tanks to rise to the occasion. Furthermore, the current initiatives of the Government think-tank, NITI Aayog and other government agencies have been studied in order to provide the readers information about the policies currently in progress. Our research work also gives an insight into the initiative spearheaded by Army Design Bureau (ADB) and application-oriented research in AI undertaken by DRDO labs, highlighting the viewpoint of the Indian Armed Forces and their progress towards leveraging AI into their military operations.

A comparative study between India and the P5 Nations has also been conducted to help the readers understand where India stands today in terms of AI Strategy &Readiness and the analysis conducted sheds light on India's current standing and the progress made in the advancement of AI in military applications to bolster the vital pillar of National Security, i.e., the Armed Forces.

Keeping in mind, the ethical issues associated with the emergence of Artificial Intelligence in the global space, we have addressed the relevant concerns through the medium of public insights and viewpoints of experts on the 'Ethics of AI' and the 'Risks of AI.' The aspects have been studied well in depth by making use of prominent research organisation's study conducted for the United States Air Force, given that AI does not respect traditional national boundaries and there is an urgent need for cooperation between nations and AI laboratories across the globe to put in place AI safety regulations..

In the end, potential obstacles which can hamper the formulation of an AI roadmap have been identified and at the same time, a potential roadmap suggested in order to help overcome these challenges, with the hope that it serves as a valuable resource for all the concerned stakeholders involved in shaping the future of AI strategies for national security.

We express our greatest appreciation for Mr. Rajan Arya and his incredible team members from Pentagon Press LLP for constant support in meeting the deadlines and performing a tremendous job in designing the cover of this book, as also our sincere thanks to all those who helped us directly or indirectly in completing our research work.

We are grateful to Dr G Satheesh Reddy, Distinguished Scientist and Scientific Adviser to Raksha Mantri, for giving an insight into the concerted R&D efforts in the field. We are deeply indebted to him for penning down the foreword to this book as well, despite his busy schedule. We wish to thank our families for providing the necessary support and for keeping up the patience during the process of accomplishing this book.

Finally, with this maiden attempt at publishing the research work as a soldier in uniform that gives me immense satisfaction, I express my heartfelt gratitude to my parents for believing in me since childhood, my father Prof (Retd) Pramod Sinha for encouraging me and being the guiding light in all my academic pursuits and my wife Pallavi Sinha for inspiring me to follow my dreams as also thank and appreciate my son Aryan Sinha for being a constant source of motivation and keeping me focussed throughout the course of my research work that helped us achieve the goal within stipulated timeline.

Prof (Dr) Vijay S Khare

Col Amit Sinha

LIST OF FIGURES AND TABLES

FIGURES

TABLES

ABBREVIATIONS

AAP	Annual Acquisition Plan
ABCI	Artificial Intelligence Bridging Cloud Infrastructure
ACE	Air Combat Evolution
ADB	Army Design Bureau
ADE	Aeronautical Development Establishment
AFRL	Air Force Research Laboratory
AFSOD	Armed Forces Special Forces Division
AFSPA	Armed Forces Special Powers Act
AGI	Artificial General Intelligence
AI	Artificial Intelligence
AIH	Application Innovation Hub
AIOS	Anti-Infiltration Obstacle System
AIRAWAT	**A**rtificial **I**ntelligence **R**esearch, **A**nalytics and Kno**w**ledge **A**ssimilation Pla**t**form
ANC	Andaman and Nicobar Command
ANI	Artificial Narrow Intelligence
ANN	Artificial Neural Network
AR	Augmented Reality
AR	Assam Rifles
ARF	ASEAN Regional Forum
ARTRAC	Army Training Command
ASEAN	Association of South East Asian Nations
ASI	Artificial Super Intelligence
ATB	Army Technological Board
AWS	Autonomous Weapon System

BARC	Bhabha Atomic Research Centre
BEL	Bharat Electronics Limited
BGF	Border Guarding Force
BIMSTEC	Bay of Bengal Initiative for Multi-Sectoral Technical and Economic Cooperation
BRICS	Brazil, Russia, India, China and South Africa
BSF	Border Security Force
C4ISR	Command, Control, Communications, Computers, Intelligence, Surveillance and Reconnaissance
CAIR	Centre for Artificial Intelligence and Research
CARACAS	Control Architecture for Robotic Agent and Command and Serving
CCW	Certain Conventional Weapons
CDS	Chief of Defence Staff
C-DAC	Centre for Development of Advanced Computing
CET	Council for Ethics and Technology
CFIUS	Committee on Foreign Investment in the United States
CIDSS	Command, Information and Decision Support System
CI/CT	Counter Insurgency/ Counter Terrorism
CLAWS	Centre for Land Warfare Studies
CMC	Central Military Commission (China)
COAS	Chief of Army Staff
COP	Common Operational Picture
CORE	Centre of Research Excellence
CPU	Central Processing Unit
CRL	Central Research Laboratory
CRPF	Central Reserve Police Force
CRS	Congressional Research Service
CSS	Cabinet Secretary on Security
DAIC	Defence Artificial Intelligence Council
DAIPA	Defence Artificial Intelligence Project Agency
DAP	Defence Acquisition Procedure
DARPA	Defence Advanced Research Project Agency
DCA	Defence Cyber Agency
DCAP	Defence Capital Acquisition Plan

DCOAS (CD&S)	Deputy Chief of Army Staff (Capability Development and Sustenance)
DCOAS (P&S)	Deputy Chief of Army Staff (Planning and Systems)
DCOAS (S)	Deputy Chief of Army Staff (Strategy)
DCS	Direct Commercial Sales
DDP	Department of Defence Production
DG (CD)	Director General (Capability Development)
DG (IS&C)	Director General (Information Systems and Coordination)
DG (IS&T)	Director General (Information Systems and Training)
DGIW	Director General (Information Warfare)
DGMT	Director General (Military Training)
DG (WE)	Director General (Weapons &Equipment)
DIO	Defence Innovation Organisation
DOD	Department of Defence
DPC	Defence Planning Committee
DPSU	Defence Public Sector Undertaking
DRDO	Defence Research and Development Organisation
DSA	Defence Space Agency
DSE	Defence Services Estimates
DST	Department of Science and Technology
DX	Digital Transformation
DYSL-AI	Defence Young Scientist Laboratory-Artificial Intelligence
EW	Electronic Warfare
FET	Field-Effect Transistor
FLOPS	**Fl**oating-point **Op**erations per **s**econd
FTA	Free Trade Agreement
GAN	General Adversarial Network
GCI	Global Cybersecurity Index
GDP	Gross Domestic Product
GGE	Group of Governmental Experts
GHI	Global Hunger Index
GoI	Government of India
GPAI	Global Partnership on Artificial Intelligence

GPS	Global Positioning System
GPU	Graphical Processing Unit
HAL	Hindustan Aeronautics Limited
HDI	Human Development Index
HM	Hizbul Mujahideen
HPC	High Performance Computing
HSMC	Hongxin Semiconductor Manufacturing Company
IaaS	Information as a Service
IAF	Indian Air Force
ICDP	Integrated Capability Defence Plan
ICT	Information and Communication Technology
ICTAI	International Centre for Transformational Artificial Intelligence
IDC	International Data Corporation
iDEX	Innovations for Defence Excellence
IDF	Israeli Defence Forces
IDS	Integrated Defence Staff
IED	Improvised Explosive Device
IIIT	Indian Institute of Information Technology
IISc	Indian Institute of Science
IISER	Indian Institute of Scientific Education and Research
IIT	Indian Institute of Technology
IMF	International Monetary Fund
IOR	Indian Ocean Region
IoT	Internet of Things
IP	Intellectual Property
IPEF	Indo-Pacific Economic Framework
ISR	Intelligence, Surveillance and Reconnaissance
ISRO	Indian Space and Research Organisation
IT	Information Technology
ITBP	Indo-Tibetan Border Police
JAIC	Joint Artificial Intelligence Centre
JeM	Jaish-e-Mohammad
KCP	Kangleipak Communist Party

KYKL	Kanglei Yawol Kanna Lup
LAWS	Lethal Autonomous Weapon System
LeT	Lashkar-e-Taiba
LISP	List Processing
LoC	Line of Control
LWE	Left Wing Extremism
MAD	Mutually Assured Destruction
MAF	Ministry of Armed Forces (France)
MALE	Medium Altitude Long Endurance (UAV)
MARF	Multi-Agent Robotics Framework
MBT	Medium Battle Tank
MCTE	Military College of Telecommunication Engineering
MeitY	Ministry of Electronics and Information Technology
MI	Military Intelligence
MIS	Management Information System
ML	Machine Learning
MNF	Mizoram National Front
MoCI	Ministry of Commerce and Industry
MoD	Ministry of Defence
MOST	Ministry of Science and Technology (China)
MPI	Multi-Dimensional Poverty Index
MSME	Micro, Small and Medium Enterprise
N-AIM	National Artificial Intelligence Mission
NASSCOM	National Association of Software and Services Companies
NCERT	National Council for Education, Research and Training
NCF	National Curriculum Framework
NCW	Network-Centric Warfare
NDAA	National Defence Authorisation Act
NDFB	National Democratic Front of Bodoland
NFS	Network For Spectrum
NIC	National Informatics Centre
NII	National Information Infrastructure
NISE	National Institute of Solar Energy

NIST	National Institute of Standards and Technology
NIT	National Institute of Technology
NITI	National Institution for Transforming India
NKN	National Knowledge Network
NLP	Natural Language Processing
NSAI	National Strategy for Artificial Intelligence
NSCAI	National Security Committee on Artificial Intelligence
NSCN (IM)	National Socialist Council of Nagaland (Isak Muivah)
NSCN (K)	National Socialist Council of Nagaland (Khaplang)
NSM	National Supercomputing Mission
NSS	National Security Strategy
NTF	National Task Force
OECD	Organisation for Economic Cooperation and Development
OIS	Operational Information System
OODA	Observe, Orient, Decide and Act
ORF	Observer Research Foundation
OT	Operational Technology
PaaS	Platform as a Service
PIJ	Palestinian Islamic Jihad
PLA	People's Liberation Army
PLASSF	People's Liberation Army Strategic Support Force
PREPAK	People's Revolutionary Party of Kangleipak
QUAD	Quadrilateral Security Dialogue (QSD)
RASP	Recognised Air Space Picture
RM	Raksha Mantri
RMA	Revolution in Military Affairs
RPA	Remotely Piloted Aircraft
SaaS	Software as a Service
SIDM	Society of Indian Defence Manufacturers
SIPRI	Stockholm International Peace Research Institute
SIW	Strategic Information Warfare
SMAC	Social, Mobile, Analytics and Cloud Services
SDG	Sustainable Development Goals

SCO	Shanghai Cooperation Organisation
SAGAR	Security and Growth for All in the Region
SAARC	South Asian Association of Regional Cooperation
SFC	Strategic Forces Command
SHQ	Service Headquarters
SSB	Sashastra Seema Bal
STEM	Science, Technology, Engineering, Mathematics
SAPIENT	Sensing for Asset Production using Integrated Electronic Network Technology
TDF	Technology Development Fund
TPU	Tensor Processing Unit
TSMC	Taiwan Semiconductor Manufacturing Company
TTRP	Technology Transformation Research Park
TIH	Technological Innovation Hub
USMC	United States Marine Corps
UAV	Unmanned Aerial Vehicle
ULFA	United Liberation Front of Asom
UNLF	United National Liberation Front
UNSC	United Nations Security Council
VR	Virtual Reality
XLUUV	Extra Large Unmanned Underwater Vehicle

1

Introduction

"The supreme art of war is to subdue the enemy without fighting."

—**Sun Tzu**

Military power or the hard power is one of the most important instruments of the government along with diplomacy or soft power and economic capacity. These instruments of power that form the concept of National Security, exist along the entire Spectrum, wherein military power is about control whereas diplomacy is about influencing and persuading others to achieve an objective. Within this strategic and geo-political context, the character of modern warfare is changing and technology has a significant role to play in this next generation warfare called 5th Generation Warfare (5GW) which is more about shaping perceptions than about combat, having increased focus on non-kinetic tools of warfare.

Artificial Intelligence (AI) is a constellation of technologies that is growing at an unprecedented pace today. The AI-based intelligent autonomous systems now possess the potential to replace the human mind in the **Observe-Orient-Decide-Act (OODA) loop** by matching the human capabilities of sense, comprehend and act, as shown in Figure 1.

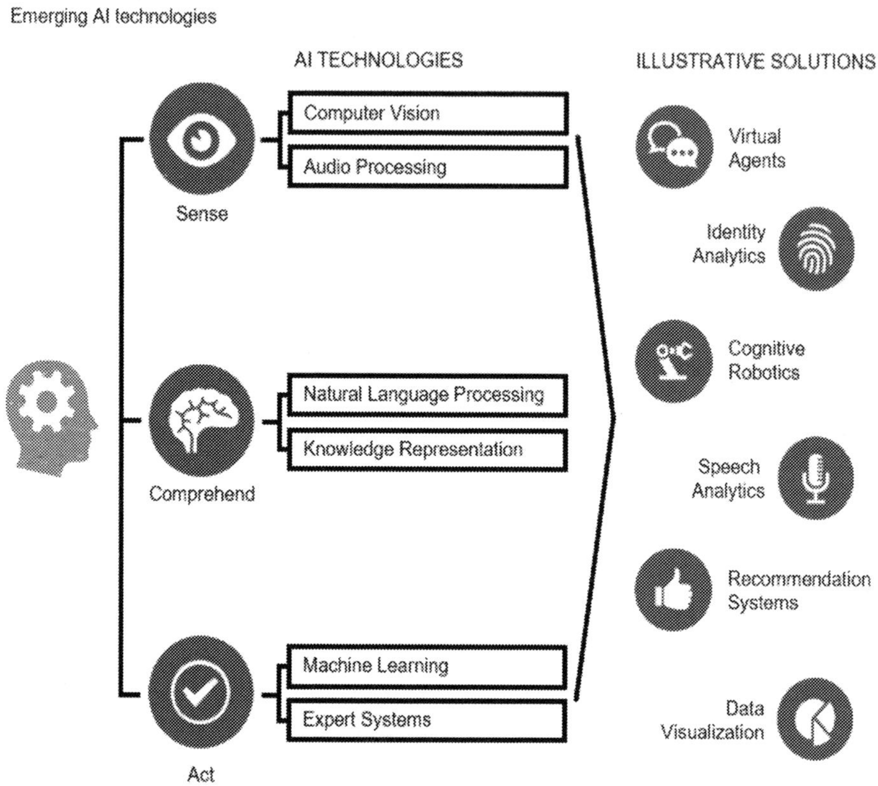

Figure 1: AI in OODA Loop

Source: NSAI Discussion Paper, NITI Aayog.

Kevin Kelley, the founder of 'Wired Magazine' compared the transitional impact of AI to that of electricity over a century ago stating: "Everything that we formerly electrified, we will now cognitise."

1.1 WHAT IS ARTIFICIAL INTELLIGENCE?

1.1.1 Birth of AI

In 1950, the seeds of AI were sown by Alan Mathison Turing, an English computer scientist, famous for his contribution in breaking the Nazi Germany's 'ENIGMA' code during the Second World War, who published a seminal paper titled 'Computing Machinery and Intelligence'. In this paper he speculated whether machines could think. He proposed 'Turing Test' to support this philosophy of AI in machines.

In the first-ever AI conference at Dartmouth, New Hampshire in 1956, John McCarthy coined the term "Artificial Intelligence". He also invented 'LISP' language, the second oldest language after FORTRAN, which became the standard programming language for AI Systems.

1.1.2 Definition of AI

AI is the intelligence that the machine demonstrates. It is an endeavour to replicate or simulate human intelligence. AI is the fusion of science, mathematics and computer science that uses complex algorithms and mathematical models to build intelligence. However, a common definition acceptable across the community does not seem to exist. Nevertheless, keeping in view, its journey from being a mere academic discipline since its birth, to being the most disruptive breakthrough during the last five years with diverse approaches to research, some of the definitions by personalities/act associated with artificial intelligence are as under:

- "AI is the science and engineering of making intelligent machines."

  —**John McCarthy (1956)**, father of AI

- "AI is the study of how to make computers do things, at which, at the moment, people are better."

  —**Elaine Rich (1983)**, Author of 'Artificial Intelligence', University of Texas at Austin

Various definitions by the **National Defence Authorisation Act (NDAA) (2019)** are as under:

- "Any artificial system that performs tasks under varying and unpredictable circumstances without significant human oversight, or that can learn from experience and improve performance when exposed to data sets."
- "An artificial system developed in computer software, physical hardware, or other context that solves tasks requiring human-like perception, cognition, planning, learning, communication, or physical action."

- "An artificial system designed to think or act like a human, including cognitive architectures and neural networks."
- "A set of techniques, including machine learning that is designed to approximate a cognitive task."
- "An artificial system designed to act rationally, including an intelligent software agent or embodied robot that achieves goals using perception, planning, reasoning, learning, communicating, decision-making and acting."

1.1.3 Historical Developments

Since its birth in 1956, AI Technology had its ups and downs, marked by **AI Summers** or peaks and **AI Winters** or troughs. A brief history of AI through the period from 1950 till present is enumerated below.

1956-1974 (1st AI Summer)

- 1950: Alan Turing creates a test to measure a machine's intelligence.
- 1956: John McCarthy at the Dartmouth Conference coins the term 'Artificial Intelligence.' Logic Theorist, the first AI program is written.
- 1956: DARPA starts funding AI research.
- 1959: Samuel Checker's program used Machine Learning to beat human players.
- 1961: IBM Shoebox performed arithmetic by voice command. Unimate, the first industrial robot was introduced.
- 1963: Leonard Uhr and Charles Vossle introduce the first machine learning program that can adaptively acquire and modify features.
- 1964-66: ELIZA, an artificial conversational 'therapist' created.
- 1965: Edward Feigenbaum introduces first expert system.
- 1966: Shakey became the first mobile robot 'aware' of its surroundings.

1974-1980 (1st AI Winter)

- 1969: Publication of 'Perceptrons', a critical review of advances in AI, marks a period of declining interest and funding.
- 1973: Lighthill Report concludes that AI discoveries are disappointing.

1980-1987 (2nd AI Summer: AI Boom)

- Commercial application of Experts Systems became popular in this period.
- Expert Systems were rule-based programme that answered questions and solved problems within a small domain of specific knowledge.
- Promise of ANI-like expert systems: Application of AI recognised.
- Interest and funding for research started with Japan's launch of 10-year 5th Generation Computer Systems Project in the year 1981. (Focus on an AI system with features like Natural Conversation, Translation and Image Interpretation).
- West follows Japan to provide suit and funding for AI research such as Microelectronics and Computer Technology Corporation (MCC) in USA in the year 1983 and Alvey Project in United Kingdom in the year 1984.
- DARPA founded its Strategic Computing Initiative with an aim to triple its funding for AI based research.
- As a result of these initiatives, software and hardware companies converged around expert systems and sales during the period 1980-1988, skyrocketed from a few million dollars to two billion dollars.

1987-1994 (2nd AI Winter)

- The boom phase busted in Japan, USA and Europe as programmes failed to meet their objectives.
- After 1987, specialised AI hardware companies failed or collapsed due to emergence of desktop computers by Apple

and IBM which rapidly outclassed more expensive AI-specific ones.

- Expert Systems proved to be of limited utility; they were ineffective, added little value (Small Expert Systems) and were expensive to create, test and keep updated as also vulnerable to crashes (Large Expert Systems).
- Leadership of DARPA stated that the researchers had once again over promised and under delivered.
- This resulted in severe funding cut across Strategic Computing Initiative, leaving only those programs of directly military relevance.

1994-2004 (AI Spring: AI revival)

- Computing power increases, algorithms improve and big data improves training data.
- 1997: IBM's 'Deep Blue', a chess playing computer beats World champion Garry Kasparov.
- 2004: DARPA grand challenge on autonomous cars starts.

2004-till present (3rd AI Summer)

- 2007: Geoffrey Hinton publishes influential paper on Deep Learning.
- 2009: Google builds its first self-driving cars to handle urban conditions.
- 2010: Apple introduces Siri, a smartphone application that uses natural language to answer questions.
- 2012: Deep Learning system wins computer vision contest.
- 2014: Ian Goodfellow devises Generative Adversarial Network (GAN).
- 2015: Baidu's Minwa supercomputer uses a special kind of neural network program beats Google and Microsoft in image recognition test.
- 2016: Deep Mind's AlphaGo program powered by a deep neural network beats 'go' champion Lee Sedol in a five-game match.

- 2018: AI's language processing model outscores humans at reading comprehension test.
- 2020: OpenAI's GPT-3 (Generative pre-trained transformer third generation) is the largest language model using deep learning to produce human-like text with 175 Billion ML parameters, introduced in May 2020.
- 2021: First AI war between Israel and Palestinian Islamic Jihad (PIJ); UN Convention on Certain Conventional Weapons (CCW) by Group of Governmental Experts (GGE) held to arrive at a framework towards regulating the use of AI-based Lethal Autonomous Weapon Systems (LAWS).

1.1.4 Convergence of Key Enablers for Sustained AI Summer

AI technology is presently witnessing the AI summer due to the convergence of following three key enablers, which serve as fuel for advancement of AI:

- The increase in computer processing power largely owing to evolution of processing units, from Central Processing Unit (CPU) to Graphical Processing Unit (GPU) to the latest Tensor Processing Unit (TPU), meant for Neural Networks.
- Exponential growth of data or 'Big Data' which is estimated to grow to 180 zettabytes by 2025 as per International Data Corporation (IDC), providing large datasets.
- Improved Machine Learning (ML) algorithms through training of large datasets, compounded by unlimited processing power (supercomputers in excess of 1 exa FLOPS or 1x 10^{18} **FL**oating-point **OP**erations per **S**econd).

1.2 CATEGORIES, TYPES AND BRANCHES OF AI

1.2.1 Categories of AI (Based on Technology)

Three main categories of AI based on technology are as under:

- **Artificial Narrow Intelligence**. Artificial Narrow Intelligence (ANI) is a set of Artificial Intelligence involving machines that can perform only a narrowly defined set of specific tasks. This classification of Artificial Intelligence is also referred to as 'Weak AI'. At this stage, machines do not possess any thinking ability. Almost all AI systems built till date fall under this category. Examples of this type of Artificial Intelligence are Siri, Alexa, AlphaGo, Sophia, self-driving cars, etc.

- **Artificial General Intelligence**. Artificial General Intelligence (AGI) is the stage in the evolution of Artificial Intelligence wherein machines will possess the ability to think and make decision just like humans. This classification of Artificial Intelligence is also referred to as 'Strong AI'. At this stage, no machines have been built in this category but it is believed that soon we will have the machines in this category.
- **Artificial Super Intelligence**. Artificial Super Intelligence (ASI) is the stage in the evolution of Artificial Intelligence wherein computers will surpass the human beings. Currently it is considered as a hypothetical situation as depicted in many movies and fiction books. This classification of Artificial Intelligence is also referred to as 'Conscious AI'.

1.2.2 Types of AI (Based on Functionality)

Artificial Intelligence is classified into following four types on the basis of functionality:

- **Reactive AI**. It includes machines that operate solely based on present data, taking into account only the current situation. Reactive AI machines cannot form inferences from data to evaluate their future actions. IBM chess program is a well-known example of Reactive AI.
- **Limited Memory AI**. Limited memory AI machines can make improved decisions by studying past data from its memory. Such an AI has short lived or temporary memory that is used to store past experience to evaluate future actions. An example of Limited Memory AI is self-driven cars.
- **Theory of Mind AI**. It is a more advanced type of AI. This classification of AI can mainly focus on emotional intelligence so that human beliefs and thoughts can be better

comprehended. This classification is still under research and it has not yet been developed.

- **Self-Aware AI**. Under this classification, machines have their own consciousness.

Such machines will not be developed by humans, but the AI machine which is more intelligent than humans can develop and replicate on its own. As described by Elon Musk, this classification is a fundamental risk to human civilisation.

1.2.3 Branches of AI

- **Machine Learning.** Machine learning (ML), a subset of AI, is the science of getting machines to interpret, analyse and process data in order to solve the real-world problems. It leverages data to improve performance on some set of tasks. Though the term was first used in 1959, it flourished only in 1980s during second AI summer. It is further classified into four types which are as under:
- **Supervised Learning**. In this type, the machine is supervised while it is learning. With example inputs and desired outputs called training data or labelled data known, the goal is to learn a general rule that maps inputs to outputs.
- **Unsupervised Learning**. In this type, no labelled training data is presented to the learning algorithm leaving it on its own to learn patterns from untagged data and find structure in its input.
- **Semi-Supervised Learning.** This type of Machine Learning falls between the above two classifications, wherein a small amount of labelled data is combined with a large amount of unlabelled data during training. It is a case of weak supervision.
- **Reinforcement Learning.** In this type, the algorithm is designed such that it does not need labelled input/output pairs like supervised learning, nor does it need sub-optimal actions to be explicitly corrected. The aim is to find a balance between exploration of something not known and exploitation of something known, i.e., current knowledge.

- **Deep Learning.** Deep learning, a subset of ML (as shown in Figure 2 below), was first referred to in an influential paper published by Geoffrey Hinton, a British-Canadian computer scientist in the year 2007. It is a technique to perform ML inspired by our brain's own network of neurons. It is based on multiple layers of 'artificial neural network' that refers to the word 'deep' in its name. It is the use of this method that revolutionised the stagnant traditional ML algorithms in 2010s leading to drastic improvement in performance of AI algorithms, as shown in Figure 3 below. Computer vision and speech recognition are applications of deep learning.

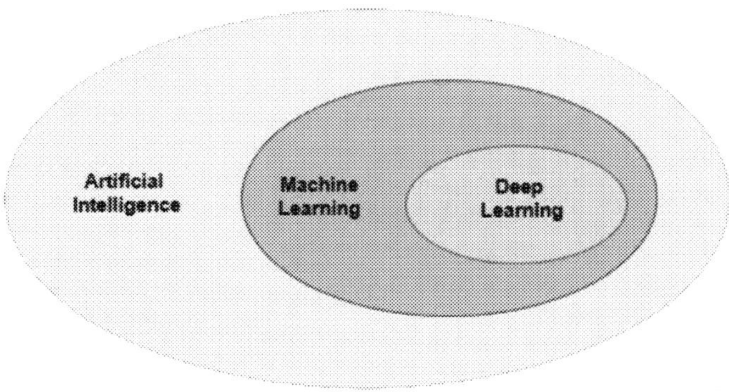

Figure 2: Artificial Intelligence-Machine Learning-Deep Learning Relationship
(ML is a subset of AI and Deep learning is a subset of ML)

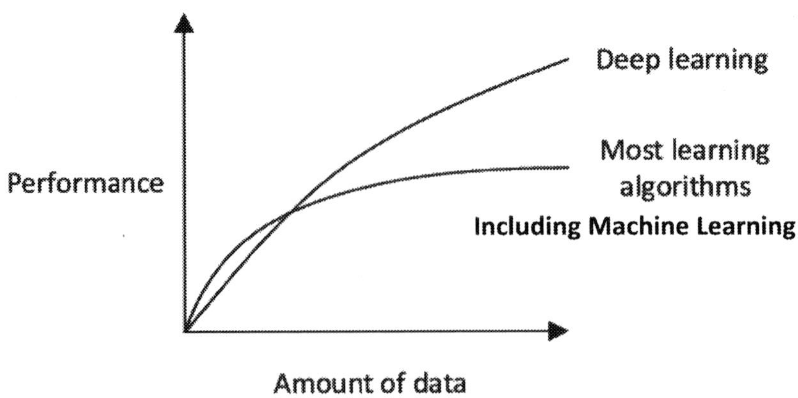

Figure 3: Comparison of Performance: Deep Learning vs. Machine Learning and other algorithms

- **Natural Language Processing**. Natural Language Processing (NLP) refers to the science of drawing insights from natural human language in order to communicate with machine. For example, Amazon uses NLP to improve its services from user review. Twitter uses NLP to block accounts with terrorist linkage, hatred speeches, etc.
- **Robotics.** Robotics is a branch of Artificial Intelligence which focusses on different branches and applications of robots. AI Robots are Artificial Agents which act in the real-world environment to produce results by taking accountable actions. An example of this is 'Sophia' (Humanoid robot developed by Hong Kong based firm Hanson Robotics and activated in May 2016).
- **Fuzzy Logic.** Fuzzy logic is a computing approach that is based on the degree of truth rather than binary logic 0 and 1. The concept of fuzzy logic is used in medical field, automatic gear system in car, etc.
- **Expert Systems**. An expert system is an AI based computer system that learns and reciprocates the decision-making ability of human experts. It uses 'if...then' logical notations to solve complex problems. This concept is used in Information management, fraud detection, etc.

1.3 AI RELATED TECHNOLOGIES AND TECHNIQUES

- **Big Data**. It is a field that treats ways to analyse, systematically extract information from, or otherwise deal with data sets, that are too large or complex to be dealt with by traditional data-processing application software. It refers to significant volumes of data, both unstructured and structured. Big Data consists of high volume, high velocity or high variety, (volume, velocity and variety being three key concepts of Big Data) information assets that demand cost-effective, innovative forms of information processing that enable enhanced insight, decision making and process automation. Some of the applications include Big Data for Financial Services used for Customer

Analytics, Compliance Analytics and Fraud Analytics, Big Data in Communications and Big Data for Retail.

- **Data Science.** Data Science is referred to as an intersection of automation, analytics and prediction. It deals with unstructured, semi-structured and structured data. It involves the steps of data cleansing, data preparation, aligning and analysis. It can be further explained as the combination of statistics, mathematics, programming and problem solving. It includes various techniques used when extracting insights and information from data. The applications include Internet Search, Digital Advertisements and Recommendation Systems.
- **Data Analytics.** Data Science is the science of examining raw data to draw an inference. It involves applying an algorithmic or mechanical process to derive insights and running through several datasets to look for meaningful correlations. The focus of data analytics lies in inference, which is the process of deriving conclusions, solely based on what the research already knows. Applications are in various fields such as healthcare, travel, gaming and energy management.
- **Cloud Computing.** Cloud Computing is a technological paradigm that is certain to be a new engine of the global economy. It is a mix of software-enabled resources and services that can be delivered to the user on an "as-needed basis".

As per National Institute of Standards & Technology (NIST), "Cloud Computing is a model for enabling ubiquitous, convenient, on-demand network access to a shared pool of configurable computing resources, e.g., networks, servers, storage, applications and services, that can be rapidly provisioned and released with minimal management effort or service provider interaction. Government of India (GoI) Cloud Initiative provides an opportunity for India's Information Technology (IT) and Information Technology enabled Services (ITeS) sectors by opening up a new avenue of providing cloud-based services to global organisations ranging from SaaS (Software as a Service) based application services, to remote application hosting services such as PaaS (Platform as a Service) and IaaS (Information as a Service).

On 12 April 2017, the Ministry of Electronics and Information Technology (MeitY) issued guidelines on setting up of IT infrastructure by government departments using Cloud Computing technology with a mandate to store entire data within the country. The National Cloud Meghraj, the home-grown cloud also called Government NIC Cloud as it is managed by National Informatics Centre (NIC), is the result of such an initiative.

Edge computing is another technique that differs from Cloud computing in that it is used in remote locations to process time-sensitive data, reducing latency and bandwidth usage. The differences between the two computing methods are enumerated below:

Table 1: Difference between Edge Computing and Cloud Computing

Edge Computing	*Cloud Computing*
• Used to process time-sensitive data and reduces latency.	• Processes data that is not time-driven.
• Preferred in remote locations where there is no or limited connection to a centralised location. Local storage required is similar to mini data centre.	• Preferred in locations with ready connection to a centralised or mega data centres.
• Beneficial to specialised intelligent devices, akin to PCs but are not regular computing devices. However, does not provide immediate response which is a major drawback of edge computing.	• Works on regular computing devices designed to perform multiple functions.

- **Internet of Things.** Internet of Things (IoT) enables us to connect "things" to the Internet and, to networks that use Internet Technology. It is a collective term for connected things such as smart phones, computers etc., how they communicate and transmit data, the technology enabling them and the reasons why it is done. It is the network of physical objects that contain embedded technology to communicate and sense or interact with their internal states or the external environment.
- **Quantum Computing**. This is based on the principles of quantum theory/mechanics. Quantum computers use the concept of 'Qubits' which can represent 0, 1 or both states at

the same time. It has the ability to perform more than one trillion computations per second and is capable enough to break any sort of existing encryption and substitute it with a hack-free replacement. In addition to this, quantum computing also has the ability to detect even the smallest of data tampering efforts. Experts believe that advancement in Quantum Computing can only enable AI development to proceed unhindered after 2030.

- **Artificial Neural Network**. Artificial Neural Network (ANN) refers to a computational model that comprises many processing elements which receive inputs and in return provide outputs based on predefined activation functions. These networks are inspired by the biological neural networks that constitute human brains. They are models based on a collection of connected units or nodes called artificial neurons, which loosely model the neurons in a biological brain. It consists of three components: input, weight or threshold and output. It may consist of a minimum of one layer; however three layers are at least required for deep learning.
- **Generative Adversarial Network (GAN).** It is a generative model using deep learning methods, wherein various neural networks compete with one another in order to predict results with an enhanced accuracy. Under this, two neural networks are put against one another via a cooperative zero-sum game, an adversarial framework, to learn. One is called the generator and the other discriminator. It was first devised by Ian Goodfellow in the year 2014.

1.4 DEFINITION OF NATIONAL SECURITY BY DIFFERENT AUTHORS

- "A nation has security when it does not have to sacrifice its legitimate interests to avoid war, and is able, if challenged, to maintain them by war."

  —**Walter Lippman, 1943**

- "The distinctive meaning of national security means freedom from foreign dictation."

  —**Harold Lasswell, 1950**

- "National Security objectively means the absence of threats to acquired values and subjectively, the absence of fear that such values will be attacked."

  —Arnold Wolfers, 1960

- "National Security is the ability to preserve the nation's physical integrity and territory; to maintain its economic relations with the rest of the world on reasonable terms; to preserve its nature, institution, and governance from disruption from outside; and to control its borders."

  —Harold Brown, U.S. Secretary of Defence, 1977-1981

- "National Security is an appropriate and aggressive blend of political resilience and maturity, human resources, economic structure and capacity, technological competence, industrial base and availability of natural resources and finally the military might."

  —National Defence College of India, 1996

- "In Indian context, National Security may be defined as safeguarding the national borders and maintain peace and stability against the external threats, maintain a stable and secure internal situation, ensure safety, security and freedom of its citizens, and promoting economic development, achieving sustained development goals, providing job opportunities, energy and environmental security and access to latest and cutting-edge technology."

  —Lt Gen Phillip Campose (Retd), 2018

1.5 DEFINITION OF RELATED TERMS

- **Strategic Autonomy.** Strategic Autonomy is a policy objective of the European Union (EU) under the Ursula Von Der Lengen Commission. It is defined as the ability of a state to pursue its national interests and adapt its preferred foreign policy without depending heavily on other foreign states.

- **Strategic Stability.** Strategic Stability is a state of affairs wherein countries are confident that their nuclear-deterrent capability would not be undermined by their nuclear-armed adversaries using nuclear, conventional or other non-conventional means. This concept is built on the assumption that stability is achieved by the fear of Mutually Assured Destruction (MAD).

- **AI Strategy.** AI Strategy is defined as a policy document that clearly lays down the objective of supporting the development of AI technology and communicates ways and means to maximise the benefits of AI for society while minimising socio-economic problems. It also lays out opportunities and challenges faced by different parts of government resulting from AI development. A unified plan can thus be offered to deliver multi-disciplinary, multi-sector and multi-actor solutions to these. Any document that does not focus predominantly on AI cannot be called an 'AI Strategy' such as an 'Innovative Strategy' or 'Digital Strategy'.
- **Dual-Use Technology.** Dual-Use refers to technology that can be used for both peaceful (non-military or civilian) and military aims.
- **Use Case.** Use case is a term used in Software and Systems Engineering to describe how a user uses a system to accomplish a particular goal.
- **Fifth Generation Warfare.** Fifth Generation Warfare (5GW) is the warfare that is conducted primarily employing non-kinetic military actions such as social engineering, cyber attacks and misinformation, which is made possible through emerging and disruptive technologies such as artificial intelligence and AI-based fully autonomous systems. The term was first used in 2003 by Robert Steele.

1.6 IMPORTANCE OF THE RESEARCH TOPIC

In the last decade, Artificial Intelligence and its sub-domains have penetrated every aspect of human lives, being an all-pervasive technology. Its dual use nature, with applications in both civilian and military domain, has driven the whole world to embrace the technology as early as possible. The timely steps taken by some developed nations in terms of government policies, drawing strategies, enhancing infrastructure and honing technical skills suggest that they all want to increase the pace of AI adoption to have a competitive edge and support National Security objectives.

India has joined this bandwagon too, albeit a bit late. The research topic becomes relevant and important here as it encompasses gauging the current global trends vis-à-vis India's status and standing today and recommending important AI strategies for National Security so as to maximise the late-mover's advantage.

1.7 OBJECTIVES OF THE RESEARCH

The objectives of the research include the following aspects:

- To study the historical developments and current status of AI Technology.
- To study and analyse the National Security threats and challenges and changing character of war.
- To study the relevance and use of AI Technologies for achieving National Security objectives.
- To study the global trends in AI strategies and views of the Government think tank, NITI Aayog.
- To suggest a feasible Roadmap of Important AI strategies for National Security.

1.8 LIMITATIONS OF THE STUDY

India having just joined the AI bandwagon, the discussion paper and approach documents on the subject, 'AI for All', by the Government think tank, NITI Aayog, have been studied. India, being in the nascent stage of embracing the technology and owing to very limited knowledge of various aspects related to AI Technology in the environment, the structured questionnaire has been done away with. However, based on 'public attitude survey' and 'experts' opinion survey' related to 'Ethics of AI' and 'Risks of AI' respectively, conducted by a prominent research organisation, responses forming top three factors in each of the two surveys, have been highlighted. Also, AI readiness and current status of AI use for military applications have been discussed for P5 nations along with India.

1.9 SCOPE OF THE STUDY

Scope of the study is restricted to AI Strategies of India and P5 Nations i.e., China, France, Russia, UK and USA.

1.10 RESEARCH METHODOLOGY

The research methodology follows a mixed pattern of qualitative and quantitative approach, and includes historical, descriptive and content analysis. Various important data related to AI readiness on the global platform have been referred to and analysed to recommend the Indian roadmap of important AI strategies for national security. Interaction with Army Design Bureau and DRDO has led to clarity on AI projects in pipeline and AI technology being amalgamated into various use cases and problem definition statements identified by Army.

1.11 REVIEW OF LITERATURE

Literature Review is an integral part of research and an important step to systematically identify and analyse a document in a particular field of study. It assists in finding the level of research conducted in a particular area of interest or study and what further course of action can be taken with respect to the subject. A critical summary of all the research articles and literature scanned during the survey in the initial part of the research has been brought out in Chapter 2.

1.12 CHAPTERISATION

The introductory chapter elucidates the terminology of Artificial Intelligence bringing out its definitions, its historical developments, categories and sub-domains. Artificial Intelligence is not a standalone concept but a fusion of many disciplines and a constellation of technologies. The associated techniques and technologies that have spurred its renaissance have been defined. National Security, the term falling within the conceptual framework has also been amply highlighted with a series of definitions from different authors. Artificial Intelligence being a dual technology has potential to shape the future wars.

Chapter 2 contains the '**Review of Literature**' within the conceptual framework. A plethora of research articles, studies, reports and books have been scanned to understand the concept and the importance of Artificial Intelligence towards developing an AI Strategy and the use of systems and techniques under Artificial Intelligence to bolster the economic and military strength of the country. A critical summary of the surveyed literature has been brought about in this chapter.

Chapter 3 titled '**Artificial Intelligence and National Security**' deals with the changing character of modern warfare highlighting the concepts of Hybrid Warfare and Grey-Zone Tactics. "Algorithmic Warfare" has been introduced in this chapter and is poised to upend Network-Centric Warfare Concept. The threats, challenges and opportunities have been elucidated as part of national security scan wherein internal, regional and global security has been discussed. The requirement for 'National Security Strategy (NSS)' has also been analysed in light of formulating the AI strategy with the introduction of the latest Defence Acquisition Procedure (DAP) 2020 document by the Ministry of Defence (MoD), that mentions its requirement for planning process.

Chapter 4 titled '**India and Artificial Intelligence: Key Initiatives** highlights the role of government in initiating the process of formulating National Strategy on AI (NSAI) in 2017 by constituting a task force to recommend the way ahead. The recommendations of the NTF and the groundwork laid by NITI Aayog, the government think tank, through discussion papers on NSAI and later the approach documents on 'Responsible AI' have been analysed in detail. In tune with 'National Security' domain, one of the 10 domains identified by the AI NTF, the use of AI for defence applications and AI Use Cases with the focus on DRDO, ADB and Indian Army initiatives have also been highlighted.

Chapter 5 titled '**Comparative Study: India and P5 Nations (China, France, Russia, UK and USA) in the context of AI Strategy, Readiness and Use in Military Applications**' gives an overview of AI Strategies and current AI Readiness Index of P5 Nations and India to gauge the status of India vis-à-vis early birds as regards embracing AI for National Security Objectives. The comparative study with the help of statistics and data collected from various reliable sources brings out the heartening fact that India is catching up with at least one of the P5 Nations on AI Readiness and overall rankings can only get better from the point where India is positioned today.

Chapter 6 titled '**Roadmap: Important Strategies of AI for National Security**' is the concluding chapter which highlights ethical concerns felt globally with respect to the use of AI-based Lethal Autonomous Weapon Systems (LAWS). The potential challenges that have been identified as potential barriers to the AI strategy that India needs, have been briefly discussed before articulating the recommendations on Roadmap of Important AI Strategies for National Security. Based on priorities and progress on various initiatives and missions undertaken by the government, the objectives have been recommended to be achieved under three different time-frames, i.e., short-term (by 2025), mid-term (by 2030) and long-term (by 2035).

2

Review of Literature

2.1 INTRODUCTION

This chapter brings out the review of literature and critical analysis of documents within the conceptual framework of the research. The concept of National Security and the requirement of NSS to chart the general direction in which the nation should forge ahead to achieve its goals are essential to this study. To understand these, related literature was scanned to gain an insight into these concepts. Also, to gauge the disruptive and all-pervasive nature of AI and its game-changing capability to revolutionise a wide range of sectors, primarily business sectors, besides augmenting the capabilities of non-kinetic warfare or special operations, a widespread survey of literature ranging from books, articles and research papers published in journals and newspapers, reports and surveys of reputed research organisations, foundations and institutions such as Defence Research and Development Organisation (DRDO), Department of Defence (DOD), Congressional Research Service (CRS), Centre of Land Warfare Studies (CLAWS), Stockholm International Peace and Research Institute (SIPRI), Observer Research Foundation (ORF), Oxford Insights, Statista, Heritage Foundation, Routledge Group, Analytics India Magazine and many other reputed online platforms to uncover insightful literature appropriate to the objectives of this study was conducted. A critical summary of the related literature, a total of 15 of them, found apt within the conceptual framework during the course of work, is presented below.

2.2 Kim R Holmes (2015) examines and provides a clarification on National Security and related concepts. Clarity on these can only help draw a NSS. The historical schools of thought on the concept dating back to the 17th and 18th century relate to national sovereignty and being ruled by international law for common good respectively. The term 'National Security' incorporates concepts like power, military strength, force and national defence. While first half of the 20th century saw military security synonymous to national security, the concept expanded over time. It now means different things to different people or nations. Some of the non-military aspects of National Security are political security, economic security, energy security, homeland security, cyber security and environment security, among others. The author clarifies not all things be meaning national security definitions or aspects to all people. It is something that should decide both what the government is expected to do and what it should not do. Military power and diplomacy are not interchangeable and there cannot be a trade-off between the two. The hard fact is that diplomacy is ineffective without military power. NSS should conceptually incorporate how the nation wants to attain national security and serve as a reliable guide for strategic planning.

The article clearly aims to warn nations that whatever non-military ideas of national security are nurtured, military power and military personnel cannot be undermined in the garb of "Whole of government approach" or need to "rebalance" or "streamline" a way out of need for military capacity. This is an eye opener for India where every self-styled strategic thinker undermines the requirements of military power in the garb of lopsided analysis of defence expenditure and lowering the morale of the forces with fatuous comparisons or incoherent concepts.

Though the article throws light on current trends in the USA, it sounds a warning bell for our nation too which is yet to come up with a NSS to chart its progress towards achievement of set goals. It clearly shows indecision and lack of understanding the concept of National Security. Apart from being a vibrant democracy, strategic heft also counts.

2.3 David J Lonsdale (2004) focusses on Information Age and maintains that humanity is entering its third wave of civilisation after agriculture and industrial wave, and that happens to be the "Information Wave". The book analyses in detail the challenges posed by Information Age to the Clausewitzian Nature of War. The author reveals the new concept, termed as "Information Sphere", the fifth geostrategic discussion to add to the land, air, sea, and space. Clausewitzian concept of war argues that technological change may change the character of war but it cannot alter the nature of the war. There is a difference between nature and character of war. War has a universal element, the objective nature which persists irrespective of any issue including technology and the other, subjective nature is what is meant as: "Character of War". This is highly dynamic and variable.

Information Warfare and its impact on war and strategy in light of proliferating Information Technology forms an integral and essential component of Revolution in Military Affairs (RMA) and is fuelling the revolutionary change that is occurring. The future battle space and the age of Artificial Intelligence and Networks seriously threaten the Clausewitzian Theory of War. Clausewitz, the Prussian General, stressed on moral and political aspects of war. He used the term "military genius" to describe individuals with outstanding qualities to excel in command and maintained war is a human activity. While intuitive ability of a Commander is given prominence by Clausewitz, Sun Tzu's ideal commander relies on caution and measured calculation. Thus, Sun Tzu's work is touted as more relevant to Information Age than Clausewitz.

AI commander in the Information Age is believed to make decision-making quicker, not susceptible to psychological pressure and emotions, can attain good knowledge of great commanders in the past and have no service or national bias to serve well as the commander of joint or multi-national forces. Further, it will be beyond ill health or fatigue in the battlefield in contrast to human limitations, both physically and mentally. However, computers forming the basis of AI, have weaknesses too, they can suffer from viruses and bugs, cannot understand the complexities and changing dynamics of politics and policies, cannot motivate men in the battlefield and deal with the welfare of men under command. They cannot predict moral factors either—the human element, and lack intuition and initiative in the event of catastrophic failure due to incorrect or infected code. Thus, at best AI can play a supporting role to human commanders, who must retain their role in command.

Similarly for organisational (networks) developments of the Information Age, a pure network has no single commander and considers all individuals equal and autonomous and decision-making is through consensus and consultation. However, not all men possess human qualities such as moral courage and sufficient understanding of humanity. So rather than choosing between hierarchy and networks, strengths of both are drawn upon as a compromise leading to hybrid structure such as 'command network', which facilitates free flow of information and de-centralised decision-making, but retains basic hierarchical ethos.

Finally, the author believes, the most substantial challenge to the nature of war will be through Strategic Information Warfare (SIW), which is the ability to bypass enemy ground forces to strike directly at the perceived centre of gravity, e.g., National Information Infrastructure (NII), instrumental aim being to create strategic effect via disruption rather than destruction. Sun Tzu's strategy matches this aspect—achieve victory without battle, and displaces Clausewitz's emphasis on the deadly clash of armies amid fog and friction. The infosphere is the fifth dimension of strategy, through which information power operates. However, information power has both advantages (a force multiplier to combat) and limitations (vulnerabilities of space systems). Thus, information forms just one dimension of strategy. Though current RMA influences changes to the character of war, such as digitisation, hybrid command structure and SIW, they must be exploited, however, they do not change the immutable nature of war.

Clausewitz Theory clashes with Sun Tzu's theory on Nature of War. The latter holds proximity to the theory of war in Information Age. A decade and half down the line, since the penning of this article, AI prowess is getting more and more pronounced and convincing with exponential growth in associated technologies. However, as computing power has gone beyond human processing by 10 times, the author's apprehensions and convictions are still true and a matter of concern as ethics and moral issues crop up on AI-based AWS and their use in military applications. Hence, AI and networks may well be suited for underpinning the human decision-making and not be trusted for independent decision-making which may lead to potential catastrophic consequences.

2.4 Kenneth Payne (2018) draws a fascinating parallel between two revolutionary developments, the nuclear weapons and the Artificial Intelligence Systems, particularly ones employing "deep learning" methods. While nuclear strategy was described as the "**first offset strategy**" by the US against their arch rivals, the USSR, to compensate for disadvantages in conventional weaponry, and information technologies as the "**second offset strategy**", AI is now heralded as the "**third offset strategy**" in the USA.

The analogy between the two technologies is owing to the fact that they have the potential to transform strategy and drastically affect the balance of power. But there are some differences too. Nuclear weapons are less revolutionary than AI, as they do not alter the psychological essence of strategic affairs.

AI, with its algorithms can shape all conflicts from lowest to highest intensity. AI research is making waves in civil applications; however, defence applications are on the rise leading to important strategic implications in near future. At present many AI technologies in military domain are still maturing, but autonomous and intelligent platforms are becoming abler to manoeuvre tasks with precise employment of force. The distribution between human and AI is getting blurred by recent advances.

The author has drawn some parallels as well as differences between AI and Nuclear capability. Among similarities, firstly both are highly technical scientific developments, requiring expertise; secondly 'revolution' is concentrated in a few states, coupled with secrecy in research and inherent technicalities, constraining public debate. Thirdly, there are valid ethical and legal concerns about related weapons and fourthly, both have the potential to transform strategy rapidly. Lastly, both have devastating consequences arousing intense debates.

However, among differences with AI, in contrast to nuclear weapons, there is no covert attempt to achieve an objective, but a more disparate research programme. Research is more concentrated in the private sector and university-based entities, and less related to military force. Unlike nuclear technologies, there is no distinction between civilian and military research in AI. On ethics front, a strong taboo against the nuclear weapons has existed since their first use. With AI, it has centred on the issues of control and accountability. On arms control front, nuclear weapons are prohibited by international treaty with limitations and restrictions on new types of warheads. Arms control idea for AI is in its infancy as the technology is still growing, though rapidly. Norms and then law will likely follow once technology matures, as these are early days. On social front, the societal impact of AI will be more profound than that with nuclear revolution, going beyond military issues. On strategic front, the strategic thinking about AI is immature compared to that about nuclear weapons. In contrast to nuclear weapons which favour defence, AI still favours the offence, given its speed, precision, acquisition and analysis of unbiased knowledge.

Finally, the author concludes that humans can impose rules of engagement, as policy makers possess a distinctly human rationality. Human psychology is not necessarily a weakness in adopting effective strategy. Taking emotion out of strategy is not possible. With AI, it will be possible, bringing out AI's true radicalism and also its greatest risks possibly.

2.5 Professor Peter Stone (2016) as the chairperson and others forming part of an inaugural seventeen-member study panel, comprising AI experts from academia, corporate laboratories and industry, and AI-savvy scholars in law, political science, policy and economics, produced this report, the first in the planned series of studies and investigation of the AI field, that will continue for at least a century. This 100-year study, with the first report published on September 6, 2016 is modelled on an earlier initiative informally known as Association for the

Advancement of AI (AAAI) Asilomar study in 2008-09 on near term AI developments, long-term possibilities, legal and ethical concerns. The standing committee preserving this 'One Hundred Year Study' will form a panel every five years to assess the current state of AI and potential societal impacts on jobs, the environment, healthcare, public safety, transportation, community engagement and government. The theme chosen was focussed on '**AI and Life in 2030**' to recognise that AI's various uses and impacts will not occur independent of other societal and technological developments.

With the selected theme to focus on 'life', military applications and AI for defence and warfare, which are deemed to potentially negate the stable developments and deployments, were kept outside the scope of this inaugural report.

In the first section, the panel defines AI as a science and a set of computational technologies that are inspired by the human nervous system and bodies to sense, comprehend and act, but typically operate quite differently from them. As per Mils J Nilsson, it is that activity which is devoted to making machines intelligent and intelligence is that quality that enables an entity to function appropriately and with foresight in its environment. An operational definition based on what AI researchers do, states—'AI is primarily a branch of computer science that studies the properties of intelligence by synthesising intelligence. The study believes that in contrast to the frightening futuristic portrayals of AI in films and novels which are fictional, in reality AI is changing our daily lives for the better.

In section II, developments of AI in various domains in the last fifteen years have been discussed. These domains are: Transportation, Healthcare, Robotic Service, Education, Public Safety and Security, Employment, Entertainment and Workplace.

Section III deals with the Current and Future AI Policy, recommending that in view of the profound changes that AI Technologies have potential to bring in, more and tougher regulations that stifle innovation, will be counter-productive, hence these be formed so as to benefit the society as envisaged.

The initiative of a 100-year study is a positive step in the field of AI and an analysis brings to the fore the reason for this could possibly be the exponential growth, the field of AI has witnessed in probably the longest AI summer presently, since its inception in 1956. It indicates AI is there to stay and bring about drastic improvements in the way we live in next 15 years. However, it is expected that AI in defence will also be considered when the study panel meets in coming years over a century, to chart the path and the extent to which it is safe to proliferate in military domain, so as not to threaten human existence.

2.6 Lt Gen DS Hooda (March 2019) entrusted with the task of formulating a draft on National Security Strategy makes a diligent attempt in preparing the report with inputs from experts in various fields such as governance, internal security, diplomacy, defence, intelligence, economics, media and social sciences. Keeping in view, India's strength as a growing power and also its difficulties that hinder its realisation of true potential, the report suggests solutions to look to the future and shape a safer and prosperous India.

The national security objectives include protecting India's national sovereignty, the territorial integrity, promoting the rise to its rightful place in international affairs, ensuring a peaceful internal environment within the country and creating a just, equitable, prosperous environment, shielding our people from risks to life and livelihood. The tenets of our NSS flowing from the above objectives that lay down the holistic national security for India are:

- Assuming our rightful place in global affairs.
- Achieving secure neighbourhood.
- Peaceful resolution of Internal Conflicts.
- Protecting our people.
- Strengthening our capabilities.

The path towards achievement of the above fundamentals is described in the report. The challenges in terms of extreme poverty, gender inequality and income inequality, all below par from global average need to be tackled to achieve real security. Capabilities in domains such as Military, Indigenisation in production, Cyber, Nuclear,

Space and Strategic Communications need to be enhanced. The report concludes with the belief that in pursuance of strategy despite challenges faced, if basic tenets are followed, progress is assured. As analysed by Sushant Sareen (ORF/12 April 2019), National Security has acquired a political salience in wake of Pulwama suicide bombing and Balakot air-strikes. This recommendation or draft on NSS is an outcome of the 2019 election manifesto by the Congress Party which has dealt with the National Security more comprehensively than its 2014 manifesto. Likewise, BJP's 2014 manifesto was more extensive on National Security than its present one in 2019, which raises an obvious question that parties in opposition show more inclination towards a holistic view of National Security than the ruling ones.

It is high time the 'ruling party' rose to the occasion this time, shrugging off indecision and adhocism in the interest of the nation, keeping in mind the importance to dovetail AI strategy formally into the document, and fulfilled the long standing requirement of the most important guide to National Security, before it is too late.

2.7 The Congressional Research Service (CRS) document (November 2020) on Artificial Intelligence and National Security, originally written by **Daniel S Hoadley of USAF** and updated by **Kelley M Sayler, Analyst in Advanced Technology and Global Security,** prepared for Members of the US Congress, in its institutional role, gives an insight into the rapidly growing field of AI with significant implications for National Security. Towards this end, USA and leading nations like China and Russia are focussed on AI and have increased their pace for faster adoption in military applications.

The document highlights various issues such as ones before the Congress, who called for national level effort to preserve the technological edge in the field of AI, over its potential rivals China and Russia. Other issues discussed are AI applications for Defence, Military AI integration challenges, AI opportunities and challenges and AI's potential impact in combat.

AI has withstood two AI Winters, during which AI progress slowed significantly and the resurgence in the present millennium is a result of enormous developments of three enablers i.e., big data, improved machine learning algorithms and increase in computer processing power. However, rapid advancements have been only in Narrow AI or Weak AI and, it will still take decades to advance in General AI or Strong AI. Still, this category has propelled investments manifold, from $600 million in 2016 to $2.5 billion in 2021. A classified AI strategy by DOD includes establishing a Joint AI Centre (JAIC), which coordinates efforts to develop, nurture and transition AI Technology to operational use, publishing a strategic roadmap for AI developments, fielding and establishing a 'National Security Commission on AI' to conduct a comprehensive assessment of military relevant AI technologies and recommendations for enhancing competitiveness.

AI research is underway in the fields of intelligence collection and analysis, logistics, cyber operations, information operations, command and control, semi-autonomous and autonomous vehicles. Deep Fake Technology as part of Information Operations is feared to be used against USA for generating false reports, erode public trust and blackmail diplomats. Similarly, military leaders have expressed concerns about the prospect of fielding Lethal Autonomous Weapon Systems (LAWS) despite laid down policy, which needs to be revisited.

On the issue of Military AI Integration challenges, unlike nuclear technology, the Global Positioning System (GPS), and the internet, wherein these were first developed by government-directed programs and later spreading to the commercial sector, AI investment though initiated by DARPA had slower progress and, riding on past government funded research, commercial companies are leading AI development, only to be followed by DOD for military applications. Also, challenges related to technology, process, personnel and cultural impede the adoption of AI for military purposes.

On the issue of international competitiveness, USA feels that ceding leadership in AI developments to China and Russia will have grave consequences for National Security, besides being at a technological disadvantage. AI has consistently been identified as an "emerging and disruptive technology" since 2016. Intelligence Agencies have asserted that implications of adversaries' abilities to use AI are potentially profound and broad. The document stresses on understanding the state of rival AI developments, owing to the competitors having fewer moral, ethical or legal qualms about developing military AI applications.

China seeks to seize the strategic initiative and be a leader in AI, through investments by 2030. Unlike USA, which had differences with Google on Project Maven over ethical issues, China is in stark contrast, having access to technology developed for civilian purposes. However, Chinese also have a history of industrial espionage and theft for possible access to US technology. This has been curtailed by CFIUS (Committee on Foreign Investments in the United States) reforms thereby blocking Chinese acquisitions of American chip manufacturing companies in existing strategic foreign investment regulatory mechanism.

Russia on the other hand, though has shown primary focus in Robotics, lags behind USA and China on AI development front. However, they have also released a national strategy for AI which outlines 5-year and 10-year benchmarks for improving on AI development in various identified domains. Russia has extensively used AI technologies for surveillance and information operations against USA. A technological cooperation with China is also a possibility.

Autonomy of systems incorporating AI in some form or the other was the central focus of USA's third offset strategy, which meant to provide the US Military a technological edge against global competitors. As per analysts, autonomous systems are a 'tactical and strategic necessity' as well as 'moral obligation' since they will reduce risk to war fighters and cut costs by pitching in for dull, dangerous or dirty tactics. Though AI may assist in combat through force-multiplying effect, speed and endurance combined with information superiority, predictability of AI algorithms is an issue, wherein it may go wrong in unexpected ways in terms of algorithmic bias leading to racial bias and gender bias, producing lethal effects in military context. Another issue is the lack of explainable output for their process. The third issue is exploitation through hacking of vulnerable own AI systems by the adversary.

Finally, the document explores AI's potential impact on future warfare despite not having entered the arena in a serious manner. Some experts opine that AI algorithms will reach full potential by the end of this decade and will not further proceed without significant advances in power efficiency of chips or quantum computing. Another problem of DOD is willingness of military to embrace AI. But if pace of AI adoption is not increased, US might end up with a symmetrical capability as her competitors. Another blow to the AI advantage is democratisation of AI technology which will enable state competitors and non-state actors to access this technology, being primarily from commercial sectors. However, it is believed that revolutionary impact of AI may alter the immutable nature of war. AI systems could induce a state of strategic instability, putting the defender at an inherent advantage.

Military leaders and the Congress must be convinced on implications of AI and exercise oversight of emerging AI trends. Shaping AI development trajectory will ensure that advanced technologies are in place to support US National Security and continental supremacy of the US military.

This has implications for India, towards achieving its objectives too and a well laid out AI strategy is a must to keep pace with the current technology as also with other leading nations.

2.8 National Security Commission on AI (October 2021) presents startling revelations on the advancement of AI for National Security of the USA and its global standing in the AI era. The National Security Commission on AI (NSCAI) was established based on Section 1051 of John McCain NDAAs as an independent commission on 13 August 2018 to consider the methods and means necessary to advance the development of AI, Machine Learning (ML), and associated technologies to comprehensively address the National Security and defence needs of the United States. It was assisted by the DOD in its quest to defend America in the AI Era and to win the AI competition against its principal strategic competitors.

NSCAI consisting of a bipartisan commission of 15 experts from the fields of technologies, national security, industry and academia, submitted its final report in 2021 and has ceased to exist with effect from 01 October 2021.

The report delivers an uncomfortable message bringing out the stark reality that America is not yet prepared to defend or compete in the AI era and highlights the areas where a concerted effort is required to arrest the erosion of its technological hegemony by 2030. To be AI-ready by 2025, the government needs committed partners in industry, academia and civil society.

AI revolution will impact economy, national security and warfare. AI innovation needs to be accelerated to benefit society and defend against malign uses of AI. The AI competition is a values competition and responsible use of AI will benefit humanity and build a safer and freer world. At the same time, AI systems will be used in the pursuit of power and will be weapons of first resort in future conflicts. AI is a dual use technology and protecting nation's interests against AI-enabled threats and new warfare paradigms should be top-priority.

The report emphasises a few areas where action is necessary because the stakes of the competition are very high. These areas are leadership, talent, hardware, and innovation investment. The report suggests a Technology Competitiveness Council to build strategy for the security economic and scientific challenges of AI. The leadership needs to decide on down payment to win AI era. As regards talent, National Reserve and Digital Corps need to be established to nurture technological talent, akin to growing military officers. On hardware front, the report reveals that USA is no longer manufacturer of the world's most sophisticated chips, which power all AI. Given Taiwan's proximity to China, the former being the largest manufacturer of the sophisticated chips and the latter the principal strategic competitor, a strategic blockage in the future may put National Security likely at risk, and recommends revitalisation of domestic chip fabrication with a minimum investment of US$ 35 billion enthused into the sector for shaping the future. Lastly, it recommends partnering with US companies, to support development of diverse AI applications, with a modest innovation investment of US$ 40 billion to expand R&D efforts in AI. Finally, the report also suggests scaling up digital talent in AI to understand the seriousness and need of investing and funding the mission without any hiccups so as to shape the future.

New Delhi needs to be equally serious in this context, learning from the urgency that USA has shown to grapple with the AI era, and must chart strategy to set its short-term, mid-term and long-term goals in conjunction with military, academia, premier technological institutions, private sector, defence R&D and civil society to shape its future rather than be a follower of policies and play catch-up, which may not help her cause in the long run.

2.9 Ambuj Saha (August 2019) is of the view that an understanding on AI objectives in the strategic context of India in military sector is a must for policymakers as India embarks on the AI journey. AI-enabled advancements have brought drastic changes in civil as well as defence sectors. Before this, military superiority was confined to a very few conventionally and numerically capable militaries such as those of USA, China and Russia. As time progresses and AI-enabled technologies unfold, this will matter less. As remarked in 2019 by then Chief of the Army Staff (COAS) and later first Chief of Defence Staff (CDS) of India Gen Bipin Rawat, India will be too late if the armed forces do not embrace AI soon enough.

So far, India has made a beginning with establishment of high-level Defence AI Council (DAIC) and Defence AI Project Agency (DAIPA) constituted by MoD. They also implemented the recommendation of multi-stakeholder task force for Strategic Implementation of AI in Defence by issuing guidelines to the Defence Organisations and Paying out a vision for capacity-building. NITI Aayog, the Government Think-Tank in its discussion paper titled "National Strategy for AI #AI for All" in June 2018 elucidated key challenges for AI adoption.

The author maintains that besides understanding the AI objectives in defence by policymakers, lack of critical infrastructure is one of the biggest impediments in the prospective of AI in India as also the role of private sector to provide an ecosystem to provide much needed investments and skill for AI to flourish both in civilian and military uses.

The academia-industry-policy synergy, the strategic vision regarding AI, and development of critical infrastructure are some of the ways to realise the strategic, societal and cultural implications of AI in defence. New Delhi, whose major strategic competitor is China in the subcontinent, must step up in view of progress made by China in the field, and have a central focus on achieving military modernisation through the vision, "AI in Defence".

2.10 Manish Kumar Jha and Amit Das (August 2021) decode the complexity and inevitability of AI in Military today and analyse the current trend of superiority in AI as the new concept of power, as modern warfare has turned more complex, its outcome dictated by any one of the many micro-variables.

The recent drone attack at the IAF base in Jammu is thought to be the beginning of this covert form of warfare, and such threats of unrestrained intensity, without an actual war may be the norm. Areas are being identified where AI-enabled systems can plug-in with conventional military operations. The supremacy of USA has been challenged by China by out-thinking the complete AI-ecosystem to be world leader by 2030.

AI enables faster decision-making, handling the OODA loop faster and integrating with regular military operations to carry out mundane tasks and to free up soldiers to stress more on core functions. AI has the potential to analyse a plethora of structured and unstructured data for real-time decision support. It can be used to extract strategic information hidden within the voluminous data created out of international maritime operations, to draw a smart maritime strategy.

The fusion of AI with war strategy can generate deep strategic insights for commanders to reduce war losses through highly accurate real-time predictive inputs. The authors suggest a phased AI-evolution for the military and bring out a list of potential AI based solution to enhance future combat skills. India cannot lag behind so as to be counted among frontline countries in adoption of AI for defence towards bolstering National Security.

2.11 CLAWS Issue Brief (2021) attempts to understand the relationship between Indian Army and technology to address some inherent challenges using applications of niche technologies and way ahead.

The next big revolution currently is the cognitive convergence between man and machine which can be bridged by AI, supported by large amount of training data requiring interdependence on Big Data, IoT, 5G and Cloud Computing.

Digital India Programme had a tremendous success linking technology to social development. Technology Industries and AI based start-ups are taking major strides in emerging technologies. But challenges exist in form of R&D efforts being miniscule, uncertainty on data privacy, absence of major data sets for AI systems and absence of indigenous chip-making industries.

The Government initiatives towards AI is praiseworthy taking steps in constituting task forces acknowledging strategic importance of AI, identifying areas for AI based solutions, establishing agencies DAIC and DAIPA under Honourable Raksha Mantri (RM) and Secretary (Defence Production) respectively.

The Indian Army needs to focus on automation that will ultimately lead to autonomy. A need to create a 'data-driven' culture in the Indian Army is felt so that emphasis is laid on standardisation of protocols for collecting, collating and storing data. This is because massive data is stored by different branches and directorates piecemeal and not suitable for providing training data for AI. An overarching backbone with a common set of protocols needs to be designed to contribute to the automation of support services in the Army.

The way ahead suggested is first bolstering existing capacities and concurrently create new ones to harness the fourth Industrial Revolution. The three core areas suggested to be focussed on are 'Cyber Security', 'Data Generation', and 'Inception to Action' within stipulated timelines. The Armed Forces can develop their own cloud with a suggested name 'BADAL' (Bulk Accumulation of Data for Automation and Learning).

The suggestions and recommendations are indeed practical and in tune with the requirements of emerging technology such as AI to proliferate and relieve the soldier to focus on more important core tasks. AI, however, is no more a niche technology as has been termed. Also, owning own cloud and naming it 'Bharat BADAL' has already been suggested earlier in April 2015 by LS Subramanian, CEO, NISE India in his online article in Dataquest (NISE or National Institute of Solar Energy specialises in Cloud Computing, Big Data among other businesses and technology).

2.12 Shraddha Goled (November 2020) reiterates the pervasiveness of AI in civilian industries already and becoming a critical part of modern warfare. Developed nations are making grandiose investments in R&D efforts towards equipped military systems resulting in improved self-control, self-regulation and self-actuation due to superior decision-making capabilities.

Some of the use cases of AI in defence include training, surveillance, arms and ammunition, cyber security and logistics, as appreciated by the author. The frontrunners in the use of AI in military are USA, China and Russia.

The US Defence Department released its first AI strategy in 2019 to accelerate use of AI systems in the military. Some of the significant AI-based projects deployed in the US Military are Project Maven related to Intelligence, Surveillance and Reconnaissance (ISR), Squad X Experimentation Program to design, develop and radiate autonomous system prototypes and the Offset Program, the framework for preserving the technological edge against global competitors.

China has stressed upon military-civil fusion style innovation. Some of the projects related to this fusion include National Defence Peak Technologies Laboratory by Tsinghua University and development of Blowfish A2 Model in collaboration with Ziyang UAV Company that can autonomously perform complex combat missions. China's ambitious AI plan called State Council AI plan in 2017, aims to create an AI industry worth 150 billion RMB, approximately $21.7 billion by 2020.

Russian defence aims to capitalise on AI, Big Data and machine learning to conduct more impactful information operations. Russia is currently focussed on detection, analysis and debunking misinformation.

The challenges lie in the investment, both in terms of money and skill. Ethical dilemma on AI use in defence also hinders its proliferation in defence, for fear of escalation of tension unintentionally. India needs to choose carefully in tune with its requirements, for AI development needs money, that in our own nation, is a premium, especially when a considerable population is still living under the poverty line (as per latest study in the World Bank, poverty rate is close to 10% i.e., 120-140 million people below poverty line).

One of the main goals under the Sustainable Development Goals (SDGs) is to end extreme poverty by 2030. That also coincides with the timeline envisaged for India to spiral to the largest 3rd largest economy in the world.

2.13 Air Vice Marshal (AVM) Arjun Subramanian (Retd) (2022) urges the strategic community to re-invent themselves and massively upgrade their 'strategic thinking' since intellectual power (more than the military power) challenges Beijing, in the backdrop of mounting strategic asymmetry between China and India. India's strategic and the Armed Forces community need to be at guard against the assumption that with the increasing capability, up scaled strategic thinking will follow, which is a fallacy.

The author aptly quotes the book 'Unrestricted Warfare': China's master plan to destroy America, written by two Chinese Colonels, Qiao Liang and Wang Xiangmi in 1999. The strategic idea must have been sown in early 1990s itself based on Deng Xiaoping's strategy of "Hide your strength and bide your time". Their ideas now form the basis of China's evolving Grey-Zone and Hybrid Warfare Tactics against Japan, Taiwan and India.

In combat, the author rues the fact that very few big strategic ideas flow from India's strategic establishments, its armed forces and defence-industrial complex, recalling such big thinking last originated from General K Sundarji and K Subramanyam who wrote about the likely path of nuclear deterrence that India could adopt, well before India's nuclear arsenal was operationalised. For some ideas within the closed doors, deliberately not made public to hide strength, at least one idea must be openly articulated so as to signal strategic confidence.

It is high time, senior leaders devoted more time to think strategically on future problems rather than mired with presently running agendas. The best possible outcome of strategic decision-making to serve national interests should be top priority that will only come through co-existence of wisdom which comes with experience and civilisational focus, and leveraging impatience and nimbleness of youth, combined with power of technology. The buck, to be what we want to be, finally stops at the strategic leadership.

However, the author has stopped short of being bold enough to bring out in public domain the undercurrents of so-called harmonious democratic relationship between the top political leadership and the military strategic thinkers as projected to the common man through social media. From national perspective, there may be no dearth of strategic ideas, however, what is more important is, the political leadership with their limited knowledge in military domain, must pay heed to ones coming out from military leadership and not distort them to their political advantage. After all it is the military of a nation that matters in times of crises. We need to see both sides of the coin to form an opinion on issues of National interest. A vibrant democracy needs to prevail without undermining military strategies.

2.14 Pranay Kotasthane (2021) lists at least three caveats to make one re-assess China's overhyped technological capacity as much above the rest, and about to topple the hegemony of the USA which has enjoyed technological edge till date.

Firstly, he highlights ruling Chinese Communist Party's (CCP's) self-preservation imperative to create the perception that things are under control at all times. Exaggerating its capabilities in technology and defence is also information operation aimed at other nation-states. However, many initiatives and companies have failed, contrary to CCP propaganda projects. Examples are Wuhan Hongxin Semiconductor Manufacturing Company (HSMC), projected to unleash China's first 7 nanometre (nm) foundry went bust in 2020, while Tsinghua Unigroup touted as China's leading chip design house, has failed to make any substantial breakthrough.

Secondly, he has analysed that the vested interest of the US military-industrial complex to align domestic vectors within, by overlapping China's technological capabilities being principal strategic competitor, has fired national imagination to prioritise expenditure on key technologies and their governance structure to maintain the global edge in Science and Technology.

Thirdly, the 'Opportunity Cost Neglect' that China chooses to hide while publicising benefits and successes of the technological initiatives. The odds of getting even close to USA's technological capabilities are heavily loaded against China for three reasons as under:

- China's per capita GDP is one-eighth ($1/8^{th}$) of that of USA and opportunity cost may catch up before it attains self-reliance.
- Earlier in the post-Cold War Era opportunity costs were being borne by other countries, particularly the USA. Since this era has ended, sensing the dragon's meteoric rise to topple USA technologically while being assisted by USA all this while, with the reforms to restrict movement of knowledge and capital to China, the technological superiority of China looks suddenly far from reality. The example of Alibaba's announcement of Yitian 710 server chip, a cutting-edge technology, can only be produced by TSMC foundry. USA is believed to be intervening to stop TSMC from accepting orders on the grounds that this chip might aid military applications.
- China may not attract best technological talent globally as the USA does, and this holds the key in this high-tech domain.

While we need to keep in mind the hype, we must be aware that CCP controlled Beijing, once determined to achieve a goal, has a history of resorting to overarching methods, ethical or unethical, legal or illegal, by hook or crook. USA is wary of this towards its concern to maintain its technological edge, especially AI-based system and India being neighbour of the dragon, needs to follow suit, so important to attain regional hegemony.

2.15 The Belgium-based company i-SCOOP (2021), reporting on disruptive technologies like AI, IoT, Big Data analytics and providing services for digital transformation and Industry 4.0, gives a clear insight into the interdependent trends between several technologies that are transforming the way people and businesses relate to technology. The convergence of multiple technologies such as AI, IoT and Big Data Analytics makes a significant impact with various cross-fertilisations, advancements, and next generation applications.

The first platform in the concept of numbered platforms with several platforms evolving is the mainframe computer system dating back to late 1950s till date. The second platform technology is the client/ server dating back to mid-1980s till present. The marketing firm International Data Corporation (IDC) coined the term 3rd platform to present interdependence between **S**ocial (business), **M**obile (devices, applications and broadband), **A**nalytics (Big Data) and **C**loud services, called SMAC in short, in the year 2011. This interwining or convergence of the above four entities in the SMAC or 3rd platform has enabled digital business.

The IoT, AI and cognitive systems, 3D printing, Virtual Reality (VR), Augmented Reality (AR) and Robotics known as innovation accelerators on top of the 3rd platform are accelerating digital transformation and innovation, leading to a digital transformation or DX Economy. Furthermore, the report also reveals convergence of IT and OT (Information Technology and Operational Technology) in the bridging of digital and physical worlds, a key to the fourth industrial revolution. Industry 4.0 or the fourth industrial revolution refers to digital transformation of manufacturing/ production and related industries. All four components i.e., SMAC or 3rd platform, Innovation Accelerators, Operational Technology and Manufacturing meet in Digital Transformation. AI and Big Data analytics are instrumental in next generation security solutions.

Thus 'convergence' will change applications and technologies profoundly. The key is to look at convergence from the perspective of innovation, purpose and those next generation applications of which some bring us close to fourth platform, which might include AI and IoT. When everything is connected, there are endless possibilities, which require a clear vision to avoid stumbling in the wrong direction.

2.16 Amrendra Dhari Singh (2022) examines and brings out to fore, the factors that have not been kept in sight while making performance evaluations of the DRDO which has been blamed in the past and is being held responsible for excessive dependence on defence imports in present times, being in the spotlight owing to Russia-Ukraine ongoing conflict.

Firstly, Arjun Main Battle Tank (MBT) project by DRDO achieved performance desired by the user in terms of mobility, protection and firepower as world class but failed in terms of weight compared to Russian T-90 tank. DRDO being a demand-driven organisation, it will fail to deliver within stipulated timeline if there is lack of cohesiveness and stability in the user requirement.

Secondly, comparison with DARPA is unjustified as DARPA works on "blue sky" foundational research projects independent from any requirements of the US Armed Forces and risk element of failure is acceptable. DRDO Projects being user-defined, risk-averse bureaucracy and rigid financial rules will not allow risk-taking; hence the comparison is not in order.

Thirdly, foundational research requires patience, time and continuous investments over years for ecosystem to be in place. Failures will have to be taken as stepping stone for future success to tread on the right path.

Finally, DRDO's decentralisation and embracing private sector as a partner is bearing fruit. Its technology development fund scheme is somewhat close to DARPA's concept of operation. The expanding R&D ecosystem along with growing R&D funds and emphasis on self-reliance will help achieve the vision of India as an emerging power on the global stage.

Critically analysing the above, the delay in DRDO programme, talent and innovation issue notwithstanding, the aspect of user requirements that are ambiguous and change as frequently as the appointments, will have to be looked into. In a big impetus to the defence industry, 25% of the annual DRDO budget will be reserved for private companies and start-ups, to accelerate development of cutting-edge military technology. This also breaks the monopoly of public sector in military technology development, which is a welcome change.

2.17 SUMMARY

From the review of literature chosen for this research work on the topic within the conceptual framework, it is highlighted that 'national security' concept has expanded over time, and encompasses non-military aspects also in addition to military security. Also lack of a formal National Security Strategy, despite numerous geo-political challenges India faces since independence, indicates that Indian political leadership lacks focus on national security. Hence, it is imperative that a formal National Security Strategy for India is in place at the earliest to ensure long-term strategic planning on all aspects of national security. It has also come to light that the emerging and disruptive technologies such as AI and other associated technologies will change the character of war and may even challenge the immutable nature of war. However, AI and networks can be best utilised in supporting role to human commander for faster decision-making. The field of AI is a revolution in strategic affairs. Keeping in view the future conflicts, embracing AI at the earliest will be the key and if not, the price to pay will be unaffordable.

3

Artificial Intelligence and National Security

"AI has come of age. It has migrated from a niche technical field to a major driving force of our future in our society."

—Fei-Fei Li, Former Chief Scientist, Google Cloud

3.1 AI: A NICHE, EMERGING OR DISRUPTIVE TECHNOLOGY?

It is important to define technology and understand the three terms, i.e., Niche technology, Emerging technology and Disruptive technology before we label AI as one or more of them. The word 'technology' comes from two Greek words i.e., 'Techno' meaning knowledge/skill and 'Logos' meaning Science. Technology is thus the application of scientific knowledge and tools or methods to produce goods and services efficiently and in an innovative manner, especially in the industry. The three stages of technology are described as under:

- **Niche Technology**. A niche technology is one in which the technological products are designed for a particular small area of a market.
- **Emerging Technology**. The emerging technology is generally perceived as capable of changing the status quo when introduced, replacing the current technology systems. These are technologies that are at an early stage of development and are characterised by radical novelty, relatively fast growth, coherence and developing a state of maturity over time so as to

have practical applications along with cost effectiveness and dramatic impact across various sectors, and uncertainty and ambiguity in terms of fulfilment of their technological promise. They also encompass older technologies that are figuratively emerging into prominence from a background of obscurity.

- **Disruptive Technology**. A disruptive technology is one that sweeps away the systems it replaces because it has attributes that are recognisably superior. These have the potential to redefine the way warfare is conducted or creating new types of warfare, combined with necessary organisational changes. For example, the Internet and its worldwide use have led to creation of a new warfare, 'The Cyber Warfare'.

The above description clearly brings out the fact that Artificial Intelligence is no longer a niche technology today. It has migrated to be a major driving force of our future in our society as remarked by Fei-Fei Li, an American Computer Scientist and Co-Director of the Stanford Institute for Human-Centred Artificial Intelligence and former Chief Scientist, Google Cloud. However, AI qualifies as an emerging technology, and is a differentiator for business in industry as it has resurged over the last decade after having faced two AI winters, when growth of supporting technologies and funding dwindled, pushing it into oblivion and obscurity. It has all the traits of an emerging technology with endless scope and applications yet to be unearthed as a strong AI or AGI, the second category of AI. Finally, it is also poised to disrupt the world as dual-use technology, both in civilian and military domain. It is one of those technologies which tend to cloud the Emerging Technology versus Disruptive Technology narrative. As analysed by domain experts AI can be called as both emerging and potentially disruptive technology that will revolutionise and fundamentally transform the way war is waged.

3.2 THE CHANGING CHARACTER OF WAR

The nature of war is unchanging, but its character is ever-changing. As defined by Clausewitz in his book 'On War', the fundamental nature of war is clash between opposing wills, and comprises violence and rational thinking. In comparison, the character of war continuously changes and evolves, under influence of technology, doctrine, geo-strategic dynamics, economy and culture across time and space. Technology, both military and commercial, offers distinct advantages to fighting forces by providing enhanced decision-making capabilities, Unmanned Aerial Vehicles (UAVs) and Unmanned Ground Vehicles (UGVs). The proliferation of AI, Big Data and Data Analytics, ML and Digital Twins (virtual replicas of physical devices or systems, used to run simulations) are precursors to what Chinese refer to as "Cognitive Warfare" as a new domain of war.

The current 5GW, a war of 'information and perception' as described by Daniel Abbot, encompasses Hybrid Warfare and Grey-Zone tactics instead of full-fledged wars. With emerging technologies such as AI and ML, 'algorithmic warfare' that harnesses algorithmic systems, adds to the list.

3.2.1 Hybrid Warfare

'War' is basically defined as a state of armed conflict between political communities (nation states), characterised by extreme violence leading to destruction and fatalities. 'Warfare' refers to its common activities and characteristics. Some of the types of warfare are 'conventional' and 'unconventional' warfare, 'asymmetric warfare', 'cyber warfare', 'information warfare' among others.

The term "hybrid warfare" was first used in an article titled "Future Warfare: The Rise of Hybrid Wars" by Lt Gen James N Mattis and Lt Col Frank Hoffman in the year 2005, that simplified it as fighting the 'Four Block War', adding fourth block to the already explained 'Three Block War' by General Charles Krulak, former Commandant, United States Marine Corps (USMC) in 1990s. In the 'Three Block War', while one is fighting on the first block, humanitarian assistance is being provided on the second and peace-keeping operations are in progress in the third block. The concept was expanded, adding a fourth block dealing with information operations and vying to win the perception battle.

Hybrid Warfare is described as one below the threshold of 'Conventional War'. However, its rise in no terms symbolises the decline in conventional warfare. It just blurs the boundaries and complicates the task of operational planning because of its nature to target weaknesses in conventional capabilities through convergence and combinations—its core characteristics.

In the Indian context, India has been facing hybrid war in Jammu and Kashmir for the past several decades to no avail. Employing the instrument of military power alone to tackle is thus a futile exercise as we have seen against Pakistan which has employed hybrid warfare blending conventional and unconventional methods on many occasions as part of its doctrine of "Bleeding India from a Thousand Cuts" to achieve its strategic goals. An aggressive posture of China along India's borders and in the Indian Ocean Region (IOR) may add further to instability in the region. The same was at display along India's borders during the Doklam Stand-Off in 2017, wherein a hybrid approach was followed by the Chinese inspired by their "Three Warfare" doctrine consisting of Media Warfare, Psychological Warfare and Legal Warfare. The Indian response, a measured one, in perfect harmony with Bhutan, upended Chinese Plans. However, Indian Armed Forces need to deploy a hybrid war strategy against its Western and Northern Adversaries. Cyber-attacks and information operations are key components of hybrid warfare, as has been witnessed in the ongoing conflict between Russia and Ukraine since February 2022. People's Liberation Army Strategic Support Force (PLASSF) oversees its cyber and Electronic Warfare (EW) force and may play Russia's hybrid war strategy to challenge India's national security. It is time India prioritised bolstering its somewhat weak cyber-defence and bridged technological gaps to invest heavily and imbibe disruptive technologies such as Artificial Intelligence and associated technologies, using innovative methods in Information Operations to win the hybrid warfare.

3.2.2 Grey-Zone Tactics

Grey-Zone Warfare, as the name suggests, has a peculiar nature and is also referred to as "Ambiguous Warfare". It is more commonly called Grey-Zone conflict or Grey-Zone Tactics, guided by Sun Tzu's strategy which stresses on 'subduing the enemy without fighting'. Grey-Zone tactics differs from Hybrid Warfare in a sense that it excludes from its ambit conventional or regular military forces. It may be called as a subset of Hybrid Warfare.

Grey Zone conflict exists below the threshold of violence. However, it can easily spiral into violence if the opponent abandons restrain. This distinction becomes clearer in the Indian context where India is fighting a Hybrid War with Pakistan while being engaged by China through Grey-Zone Tactics.

China has consistently but ambiguously engaged India in the Grey-Zone keeping the boundary disputes with India alive as was prominently seen in Doklam in 2017 followed by Eastern Ladakh in 2020 which still continues in a bid to drive smaller nations such as Nepal, Bhutan and Myanmar from India's sphere of influence. At the same time, China displays its enthusiasm for improving bilateral relations with India on global platforms such as the association of five major economies Brazil, Russia, India, China and South Africa (BRICS), Shanghai Cooperation Organisation (SCO) and World Trade Organisation (WTO). These contradictory actions indicate ambiguity regarding China's real intentions to contain India, perceived as a real competitor for influence in Asia, and fit the definition of perpetrators of Grey-Zone conflict.

Indian military power and diplomacy, the two pillars of National Security, dealt successfully with Chinese provocations in the Grey-Zone, during Doklam stand-off and continues to do the same in Eastern Ladakh following the Galwan face-off for the last two years since May 2020. The former Army Chief, General MM Naravane called these "trailers of future conflicts", where China and Pakistan will continue efforts to achieve their strategic aims by using "grey-zone" tactics instead of full-fledged war, in a collusive manner. The cyber and space domains have added to the traditional domains of land, air and sea, to influence the battlegrounds of the future, which are bound to be technology-intensive. India needs a comprehensive re-look at its National Security Strategy and include institutional capability to deal with Grey-Zone tactics. She cannot afford to lag behind in adoption of emerging technologies such as Artificial Intelligence and associated technologies for these technologies and AI-based systems will win future wars which will be driven by these technologies. Failure to initiate strategies to build up cutting-edge technological capabilities, will have devastating consequences.

3.2.3 Algorithmic Warfare

Algorithmic Warfare encompasses aspects of AI that can be applied to warfighting operations, and has the potential to replace major structural concepts such as Network-Centric Warfare (NCW) concepts. It harnesses algorithmic systems based on AI and ML for employments in future warfare. This data-centric approach to warfare forms the part of long-term strategy, the 'third offset strategy' introduced by Secretary of Defence (DoD), which is a framework touting AI-based algorithmic systems as a means of preserving the U.S. Military's technological edge against principal global competitors. While the term "Third Offset Strategy" no more exists, the concept still exists with the formation of 'Algorithmic Warfare Cross-Functional Team' by Pentagon. This organisation steers Project Maven that incorporates AI algorithms to comb through drone footage for actionable information to make more efficient and timely decisions based on the data, potentially relieving human analysts.

Algorithmic Warfare is a broad concept extending beyond data-analysis applications. An AI algorithm-based system defeated an F-16 human fighter pilot in simulated dogfight, demonstrated By AFRL under Air Combat Evolution (ACE) program in 2020. DARPA plans to take the ACE Program to a new level, i.e., from digital environment of modelling and simulation into the real world so as to improve human trust in AI systems. China has followed the same route a year later in 2021 and developed an AI system that defeated a top Chinese pilot Fang Guoyu of PLA Aviation Brigade, using tactics learned from him over previous simulations, coupled with speed and precision.

Other emerging applications are non-kinetic in nature, for example, one related to 'Cyber Warfare', in early stages of research. AI algorithm will be required to provide analysis, flexibility and real time learning to assist human counterparts against multi-vector and dynamically adapting cyber-attacks. However, the system needs to mature against the challenges, cyber warfare has to offer.

3.2.4 Operation "Guardian of the Walls": The First AI War

As reported by Anna Ahronheim in Jerusalem Post on 27 May 2021, the two-week war in Palestine between Israeli Defence Forces (IDF) and the Hamas during May 2021 was claimed to be the first AI war, where Artificial Intelligence was the key component and force multiplier in fighting the enemy, by the IDF. ML, data collection and analysis aided by supercomputing was heavily relied upon during the operation "Guardians of the Wall". Advanced programs named 'Alchemist', 'Gospel' and 'Depth of Wisdom' which were developed by Israeli Intelligence Officers by pioneering algorithms and code, were used during the war.

The system "Alchemist" used AI and ML to alert troops in the field to possible attacks by Hamas or Palestinian Islamic Jihad (PIJ). The IDF then used AI and intelligence to carry out precision strikes in an attempt to minimise civilian casualties.

The "Gospel" used AI to generate recommendations for troops in the Research Division of Military Intelligence (MI), which used them to produce quality targets and passed them on to the IDF to strike, some of the targets such as missile launchers that were aimed at Tel Aviv and Jerusalem, gathered in 'real-time'.

Though AI may have aided many attacks in the past, this proved to be the most comprehensive demonstration of the ability of AI to quickly and effectively gather targets using super-cognition, shorten the length of fighting and changing the course of war.

3.3 NATIONAL SECURITY AT A GLANCE: THREATS, CHALLENGES AND OPPORTUNITIES

The economic growth of a nation depends on the threats and challenges to its National Security, especially military threats, due to the economic burden nation has to face to address the instability so caused. Doing so, the Gross Domestic Product (GDP) per capita income, Human Development Index (HDI) ranking, Global Hunger Index (GHI) ranking, and Multi-dimensional Poverty Index (MPI) ranking are badly affected, which is the case with India despite being the world's fifth largest economy presently, overtaking France and UK, as per International Monetary Fund (IMF) estimates (2022). Obviously, India faces a myriad of threats and challenges solely aimed to unsettle the borders and create turmoil and obstacles in its path to development.

These challenges need to be addressed in a comprehensive and co-ordinated manner employing all aspects of National Security, primarily the 'hard power' i.e., Military Power and the 'soft power' i.e., Diplomacy, aided by technology.

India's rich heritage of civilisation, growing economy, enterprising youth workforce, strong armed forces and a strategic position in the IOR, form the basis of being a rule shaper than rule follower, essential for claiming leadership in the region and the world. Thus, there is a requirement to assess the internal, regional and global security threats, challenges and opportunities to address them appropriately.

3.3.1 Internal Security Challenges

India is already grappling with a two-front strategic situation and, Internal Security is seen as her 'Third-Front'. Some of the major internal security threats India has faced since independence are insurgency, extremism, militancy and terrorism either stimulated externally or nurtured internally. The following internal security threat vectors have majorly kept Indian Security forces occupied over years:

- Cross-Border terrorism and militancy in Jammu & Kashmir (J&K).
- Insurgencies in North-East.
- Naxalism or Left-Wing Extremism.

Jammu & Kashmir

Primarily originating from the soil of India's Western adversary Pakistan, the terror-based operation was conceived by the Pakistani president General Zia-ul-Haq, launched in the valley in 1989. The simultaneous activities of infiltration of 'Mujahideens' of Afghan and Pakistani origins under the covering fire of the Pakistan Army into Indian territories of Jammu and Kashmir and well-planned terror attacks against Hindus and Sikhs who formed minority pockets, triggered their exodus from the valley. This led to the Indian Army getting deployed in the Counter-Insurgency grid in the valley, to thwart the evil designs of Pakistan. The Armed Forces Special Powers Act (AFSPA) extended in 1990, has enabled the Indian Army to function effectively till date despite criticisms from vested interests. The terror outfits such as Hizbul Mujaheedin (HM), Lashkar-e-Taiba (LeT) and Jaish-e-Mohammed (JeM) have since recruited local Kashmiri Muslim youth using these proxy 'Tanzeems' to target minorities and political workers in the Kashmir Valley with an aim to instil fear and give an indigenous hue to the insurgency. Besides this, the 'hybrid war' along the 778 km long Line of Control (LoC) in Jammu and Kashmir with the adversary calls for an urgent adoption of AI technologies to cater for unconventional scenarios, be it smart fencing along the LoC, use of Robot sentries and hexapod robots, assisting in search and destroy missions in the valley or swarm drones for Intelligence, Surveillance and Reconnaissance (ISR) towards bolstering Command, Control, Communications, Computers, Intelligence, Surveillance and Reconnaissance (C4ISR) capabilities.

In the latest move by the Government of India, using constitutional provision, Article 370 believed to be the cause of the turmoil in the valley, has been rendered 'inoperative' by making the entire constitution of India applicable to the state of Jammu and Kashmir on 05 August 2019. J&K was divided into the territories of Jammu & Kashmir and Ladakh. While a majority of nations such as the USA, UK, France, Germany, Russia and Israel have remained neutral, citing it as India's internal affair, Pakistan and China have responded against the move. The positive effect of this move is yet to be felt in the valley and analyses from various sections echo contradictory opinions on the verdict. While one analysis from the ruling party expects that in near future CRPF will not be needed in J&K, without commenting on status of AFSPA that continues to be in vogue, seemingly an optimistic remark encapsulated in immaturity, the other from a security expert, Major General Sanjay Bhide maintains that the origin lies elsewhere and there has been limited effort to wage and win the war of perceptions. While terrorists are being dealt with adequately, the mind of the local youth, ignorant of the provisions of the Article and upset that the special constitutional status enjoyed by them has been abruptly removed, is the key for moving towards resolution. The perception war can be fought and won only through Psychological Intervention Operations by an agile Perception Management Organisation.

The recent targeted killings of ordinary Kashmiri Pandits, Kashmiri Muslims, non-Kashmiri Hindus and Muslims and individual security personnel indicates a sustained effort to challenge the attempts at attaining normalcy in the Union Territory since the nullification of Article 370 in August 2019. The Armed Forces have shown tremendous restraint in this difficult scenario when they have little knowledge of perpetrators of these targeted killings, which are being termed as 'White Collar' terrorists' or 'hybrid terrorists'. To counter this and increase chances of peace in the valley, the assembly polls at the earliest leading to the legislative and executive structure build-up is the recommended solution. However, till such time polls are conducted, the GoI must be swift and agile to respond to the changed tactics of the terrorists in J&K and start accepting the fact that normalcy has not yet dawned on the valley despite defanging the Article 370 because neither killings have stopped, albeit on soft targets, to support the "war of narrative" of terror organisations, nor infiltration from Pakistan. These "Hybrid Terrorists" can only be neutralised if ways and means exist to identify them before hand and to do that, as the Former Army Commander of the Northern Command, veteran Lt Gen DS Hooda suggests that GoI must realise and co-opt local leaders, empower local police and reach out to the youth, winning perception war, to stay ahead of terrorists in their planning and execution by being flexible enough whenever required, including the relocation of minorities outside the valley to plug the killing spree.

Insurgencies in the North-East

The North-Eastern region of India mostly comprises underdeveloped, forested and difficult terrain divided into seven states, i.e., Assam, Meghalaya, Tripura, Mizoram, Nagaland, Manipur and Arunachal Pradesh. These states are connected to rest of India through the 'Siliguri Corridor' also called 'Chicken's Neck, stretching just 20-22 kms at the narrowest section. The insurgencies springing up in all the NE states since India gained independence, primarily due to reasons like non-acceptance of merger with India, neglect of local language and customs and indifferent attitude by both state and central governments over decades has kept the situation tense in the region, with demands of independent nationhood or statehood or autonomy within the Indian constitution. A number of insurgent groups, active in each of the states in the region included tribal communities, mainly animalistic in nature, and followed Hindu as well as Christian faiths. Sikkim, in the north of the Siliguri corridor, became the eighth state of the North-East region, having merged with India on 16 May 1975.

The major insurgent groups are ULFA and NDFB in Assam, NSCN(IM) and NSCN(K) in Nagaland and Manipur, MNF in Mizoram, UNLF, PLA, PREPAK, KCP and KYKL in Manipur, to name a few. All these groups are fighting to break away from India and have an independent identity of their respective states. To maintain peace and stability in the region, the security forces enjoyed AFSPA in all states. However, AFSPA had been fully withdrawn earlier from Mizoram, Tripura and Meghalaya. The improvement in law and order in the region with renewed focus of the state and central governments alike, has now seen removal of AFSPA from parts of Assam, Manipur and Nagaland with effect from 01 April 2022, leaving AFSPA applicable fully only in 31 districts and partially only in 12 districts which is less than 50% of the total number of districts in four states, fourth state being Arunachal Pradesh. The move to reduce drastically, the total area now under the so-called 'Draconian' AFSPA, curtailing the extra powers to the Armed Forces to conduct, search, arrest and shoot on suspicion, is seen as a positive step in the right direction by the GoI and hailed by civil organisations and the public.

However, the centre having removed the "Disturbed Area" tag from a whopping 50% of the total districts in these four states, citing improved ground situation, it is strongly recommended that a conscious decision be taken to relieve the troops of the Indian Army so as to enable the re-orientation of its deployment in the forward locations along the borders and let the forces execute tasks what they are designed for. This will give semblance to the purpose for which they exist, that is guarding the international borders. The internal security of the districts where AFSPA has been phased out should be controlled by the police and paramilitary forces under Home Ministry. The areas still considered "disturbed" and under AFSPA are recommended to be controlled by the Assam Rifles that comprises some of the most experienced officers from Indian Army, to handle the nuances of the internal security situations prevailing in these areas. The Ministry of Home Affairs (MHA) and the Ministry of Defence (MoD) need to be in synchronisation on this issue to match their words with deeds.

Naxalism

Naxalism or Left-Wing Extremism (LWE) along the eastern, central and the southern parts of Indian across 10 states termed as "Red Corridor" forms the third major internal security threat to the nation. This rural belt covers parts of Jharkhand, Chhattisgarh, Odisha, Bihar, Telangana, Andhra Pradesh, Kerala, Madhya Pradesh, Maharashtra and West Bengal, in descending order of number of districts affected. A majority of population in this rural belt is poor, illiterate and unemployed, majority being tribal communities. The reasons attributed to the Naxalite Maoist movements are suppression of farmers, social discrimination, extreme poverty and illiteracy, land issues and government's lack of responsibility towards implementation of laws promulgated for tribal communities.

Over the last decade, the activities of the Maoists have been drastically controlled by security forces, which have brought down the left-wing extremism by 77% from its all-time high in 2009. The strategy of central forces and the police is to enter the enemy's territory to fight and eliminate them by prevailing strength. Sukme in Chhattisgarh and Gadchiroli in Maharashtra, the Maoist affected districts and dominated by Naxalites witnessed their elimination by the Central Reserve Police Force (CRPF) as reported last year, which augurs well for the future, promising to be a golden era in ensuring national security. However, much still needs to be done by the Home Ministry to remove this threat permanently.

3.3.2 Regional Security

India in its quest for rightfully seeking a regional leadership role in Asia has come a long way adopting 'Neighbourhood First' approach in South Asia, delivering on 'Extended Neighbourhood' with an 'Act East Policy' in East and South East Asia, a Gulf initiative in West Asia, a Central Asia initiative in a region of strategic importance ably supported by being a member of the SCO and taking steps in its strategic backyard, the IOR such as outlining SAGAR (Security and Growth for all in the Region) doctrine, joining as founding member of the US initiative, the Indo-Pacific Economic Framework for Prosperity (IPEF) along with 11 other countries on 23 May 2022 and being one of the pillars, of the four-member 'Quadrilateral Security Dialogue' or QUAD to counter the influence of China in the IOR. All these initiatives for a peaceful and stable region easily make it eligible as the principal competitor of the regional power China. India's democratic, inclusive and non-hegemonic credentials, combined with the tag of fastest growing economy in the world provide it more leverage than China. As for China's influence in the world order, it takes a beating indicating it is over-hyped for the reason that Beijing failed to convince Russia, given its proximity to Russia, to ensure that the Russia-Ukraine War gets over quickly.

India has historically maintained cordial relations with her immediate neighbours due to democratic ethos, non-interference in their affairs, rich cultural values, and contributive attitude. India started its umbilical relationships with seven immediate neighbours, Afghanistan, Bangladesh, Bhutan, Maldives, Nepal, Pakistan and Sri Lanka when SAARC was formed in December 1985 for promoting development of economic and regional co-operation. However, summits in the past years have witnessed more clashes with Pakistan than co-operation. Since 2014, the summit normally held annually since 1995 has not been held. To make up for this, India, full dialogue partner and a member of ASEAN Regional Forum (ARF) since 1996, has been promoting economic cooperation and free trade through Association of South-East Asian Nations (ASEAN) forum, consisting of 10 South-East Asian countries. ASEAN is a major partner of SCO, which is a cooperative model in fields of security, economy, finance, tourism, environmental protection, development and sustainability, having India as its member besides China. Significantly, India also shares BRICS platform with China, an association of five major emerging economies, Brazil, India, China, Russia and South Africa formed in September 2006, notably influencing regional affairs so as to establish multi-polar world order. The 14th summit will be hosted by China on 24 June 2022. China and Russia having announced on 04 February 2022 that there are "no limits" to their strong strategic partnership and no "forbidden areas" for their cooperation, including strengthening their cooperation on Artificial Intelligence and Information Security in the technology arena, the continuation of Russia-Ukraine conflict for so long, may not have been expected by China. However, both China and India have refrained from voting for UN resolutions condemning Russia's actions in Ukraine. The stand that India has maintained for at least 100 days since the war began on 24 February 2022, speaks volumes of India's strategic autonomy and her objective to project to the world that another major power in Asia takes a position parallel to China. In the forthcoming BRICS Summit, China must take the opportunity to mend ties with India, convening the Russia-India-China summit on sidelines. A return to the status-quo maintaining peace and tranquillity is the least it can do for a favourable Indian response. India also forms a part of Bay of Bengal Initiative for Multi-Sectoral Technical and Economic Cooperation (BIMSTEC) and all its seven member states are littoral to, and dependent upon the Bay of Bengal. At the 5th summit on 30 March 2022 at Colombo, Indian Prime Minister called upon all members to strive for transforming the Bay of Bengal into a bridge of connectivity, prosperity and security and making progress on the proposal of Free Trade Agreements (FTA) among member states India, Bangladesh, Nepal, Bhutan, Sri Lanka, Thailand and Myanmar. With the signing of three new agreements to boost ongoing cooperation activities in the field of criminal matters, diplomatic training and technology transfer facility, the rejuvenated BIMSTEC will contribute towards making Indo-Pacific a free, open and inclusive region. India forms a pivot of the four-nation QUAD consisting of India, USA, Australia and Japan, strategically on the four corners of the Indo-Pacific Region. QUAD was proposed in the year 2007 by then Japanese Prime Minister (Late) Shinzo Abe, to uphold "freedom and prosperity" in the Asia Pacific, and was revived after a decade long hiatus in the year 2017, showing the increasing focus on China with an aim to contain China in the Indo-Pacific Region to ensure that another Ukraine does not happen in the Indo-Pacific. The QUAD leaders' summit in Tokyo in May 2022 aimed to strengthen the global semiconductor supply chain has recognised that it has geo-strategic consequences. A resilient chain through QUAD semiconductor alliance is the key to AI development and the global technological edge.

Besides above alliances, India must continue to guard the Himalayan Tri-Junctions, eyed by China. A tri-junction is a small area where the borders of three countries meet and is militarily vulnerable at all times. It provides tremendous leverage to the military. There are four such strategically important junctions, all under Indian control and under constant threat by China as experienced in the past. These are as under:

- Siachen Glacier (India-Pakistan-China)
- Kalapani/Lipulekh (India-Nepal-China)
- Doklam (India-Bhutan-China)
- Diphu Pass (India-Myanmar-China)

In the last five years, China has repeatedly made failed attempts to breach Indian defences near these important tri-junctions and used psychological pressure and information operations against India. The recent standoff at Doklam in 2017 and Lipulekh in 2020 bear a testimony to Chinese evil designs. Currently in the wake of continuing deep confrontation in Eastern Ladakh with no signs of any de-escalation in the two-year long military confrontation with China since May 2020 despite 15 round of talks till date, India needs to further enhance its capability with latest technology for faster development of infrastructure in border areas. Significantly, the development of border areas is a major part of the Government's "Comprehensive Defence Strategy" as stated by Honourable Raksha Mantri. The Border Road Organisation responsible for enhancing the operational preparedness of Armed Forces has its capital budget enhanced by 40% to ₹ 3500 Crores in Financial Year 2022-23.

3.3.3 Global Security

By the end of year 2030, the world is likely to shift from a unipolar world to a bipolar world with China slated to overtake the United States as the largest economy and a global leader in the cutting-edge technology such as AI and other associated technologies. However, the United States may retain the status as the strongest military power if ethical and legal regulations on use of AI systems are in place. Nonetheless, the rise of India both economically and militarily, building strong strategic partnerships, particularly with USA and other QUAD nations, simultaneously breaking into the top 10 nations in AI readiness and adoption of cutting-edge technologies, will promote multipolarity (in conjunction with EU, Japan, UK and Russia) in the long run.

Going by current trends, hybrid warfare in the 5GW realm is the new norm, to include Information Warfare. AI-based autonomous systems and unmanned aerial vehicles (UAVs) will likely be selectively used and AI programs will likely have prolific use for intelligence, surveillance, reconnaissance (ISR) and decision-making in conflict situations.

The new world order is in turmoil as Russia-Ukraine crisis continues unabated leading to a spate of economic sanctions by the USA and the West on Russia. This has affected the entire world, pushing inflation to sky-rocketing proportions when interdependence is the new norm. In this scenario, the UN has proved unfit for the New World Order. The security concerns beyond military threats are growing. Analysing them and addressing their consequences is becoming vital for global security. The present scenario will witness a wider group of nations rather than P5 or G7, fit to represent the multipolar world of 21st century. This group can accommodate the known established powers like the USA, connectivity centres such as the EU and the countries with evolving global networks such as India. One viable option is to choose from G20 nations, so as to form a group that focusses only on unconventional security matters such as cyber security, climate change, water and oil crises and last but not the least, artificial intelligence technology that has the potential to change the face of war in lethal manner and much more effectively than the conventional warfare. During the G20 summit in 2019 on 'Digital Economy and AI', the Indian Prime Minister discussed leveraging the power of AI with then USA President Donald Trump. It is now time to forge the bilateral partnership on AI development between the two democracies ahead.

From India's perspective, the G20 formed in 1999, poses to be a vital platform. In a meeting of the G20 Finance Ministers in April 2022 calling for Russia's expulsion, the group was split into half, wherein 10 of them walked out and remaining 10 stayed put. That the group was formed to resolve issues, not perpetuate one, is a matter of concern. The need of global cooperation on economic front was reiterated by none other than former Indian Prime Minister, Dr. Manmohan Singh, the man behind the resolution of 2008-09 financial crises. The nations are now divided over the ongoing Russia-Ukraine crisis and locking horns in geo-political conflict. As explained by the former PM, the anti-Russia economic sanctions imposed by the USA and the EU are beginning to affect developing nations like India, Brazil, and South Africa, further contributing to rising global inflation.

India's contribution at the multilateral level is already known as the non-permanent member of the UN Security Council for 2021-22 term, the two-year tenure that the country has had for the eighth time on the powerful horseshoe table, the fourth most frequently elected UN Security Council member after Japan (11 times), Brazil (10 times) and Argentina (nine times). India now needs a non-disruptive geo-economic policy and a strategic economic self-interest doctrine alongside non-aligned doctrine. When India chairs the G20 summit in 2023, this perspective needs to be projected. A unique opportunity beckons India to re-assess its foreign policy, economic policy and geo-political strategy with the reshaping and realignment of the world order. India's national interest and national security are closely linked to maintaining her 'strategic autonomy' and balance her relations with all powers concerned. This can be possible only if domestic capacity and capability are strengthened. To become a rule shaper and don the mantle of global leadership, India requires indigenous scientific, technological, cyber, space, AI development and defence manufacturing capability and capacity. "Self-Reliance" is the national priority today.

3.4 NATIONAL SECURITY STRATEGY AND AI STRATEGY

Our great nation India will be 75 this year, since breaking all the shackles of British Rule and gaining independence on 15th August 1947. Firstly, Indian Armed Forces, especially the Indian Army, manages two and a half fronts, being in a state of constant conflict along the Northern and Western borders while tackling the internal security threats and challenges, all at the same time, indicating that the nation is faced with well-defined security challenges. Secondly, India is the fastest growing economy today having recently broken into the top five economies of the world, pushing two P5 nations, UK and France, back on the list. Thirdly, the revolution in the field of AI and its potential to disrupt the world, has seen India also jumping into the AI arena and drawing strategies aspiring to catch up with developed partner nation such as the United States of America and arch rival China. It is then a paradox that India still does not have a 'National Security Strategy' (NSS).

Initially, the absence of NSS may have provided the flexibility to Indian leaders and the Government in building the nation but its long-term absence even after 75 years of independence only shows the political leadership's lack of focus on issues of national security. Its absence hurts the country's aspirations to become a regional power and a rule shaper in the global world order. The lack of strategic culture in India has been much talked about and rightly so for a reason such as this because this shortfall blurs our long-term perspective towards achieving strategic goals. NSS is a necessity to articulate and enunciate the country's long-term goals. It will facilitate the following:

- A comprehensive plan to tackle our external threats, especially from China and Pakistan that pose a challenge to India's internal, regional and global security.
- The expectations and limitations of the bilateral and multilateral alliances such as QUAD to counter China in the IOR and India's negotiation strategy.
- The military capacity, development plan and national defence strategy to align procurement priorities of the three services as also roadmap to achieve jointness of three services including the role of nuclear deterrence.
- LAC management strategy including the placement of Indo-Tibetan Border Police (ITBP) now under Home Ministry, under command of India Army for synergy.
- Dovetailing important strategies of Artificial Intelligence, capable of serving our civilian and military requirements to achieve economic and strategic heft, so important for national security.

3.4.1 National Security Strategy: A Work Still in Progress

Unfortunately, well-articulated draft strategies do not exist, as the one drafted by Lieutenant General DS Hooda, former Northern Army Commander and his team as a part of the Congress manifesto in the year 2019. The importance of NSS also finds a mention in the newly formulated DAP 2020, highlighting that the document whenever formulated will form basis of evolution of planning process along with Raksha Mantri's Op Directives 2009. Unfortunately, Raksha Mantri's Op Directives 2009 were devoid of defence planning guidelines as mentioned in Defence Procurement Procedure (DPP). It is high time, Indian leadership comes up with a formal NSS document to start a definite direction for non-military functionaries and more importantly, for the Armed Forces to fight the 5GW with weaponised technology such as AI. The draft has been rejected once by the Cabinet Committee on Security (CCS) in 2007.

In March 2021, the first CDS, General Bipin Rawat at a talk stated that "Defining a National Security Strategy is one of the most important steps that we need to take." The Defence Planning Committee (DPC), a senior decision-making mechanism formed by the Government of India in April 2018 has been given several mandates out of which one is to draft a National Security Strategy for India. The nation still awaits this document.

3.4.2 Defence Acquisition Procedure 2020

The Defence Acquisition Procedure (DAP) 2020, erstwhile Defence Procurement Procedure (DPP), focussed on the clarion call of an "Aatmanirbhar Bharat" and "Make in India", makes a reference to both 'National Security Strategy' (as and when promulgated) in its planning process and 'Artificial Intelligence' wherein there is a provision for 'Incorporation of AI', it being a rapidly growing field of technology with potentially significant implications for national security.

The above initiative shows that the Government is conscious of the importance of both National Security Strategy and Artificial Intelligence Strategy and both may be on the horizon soon, the latter forming part of the former.

3.5 MODERNISATION AND RESTRUCTURING OF THE ARMED FORCES

India has the third largest military consisting of one of the most professional soldiers in the world, fighting since the last 75 years relentlessly on three fronts: The Western Borders, The Northern Borders and tackling the internal security challenges and threats. The aim is to guard its borders without interfering in internal affairs of other nations, be it neighbourhood or far neighbourhood while keeping its strategic autonomy intact. However, the rising economic power grapples with the dilemma of balancing its capital and revenue budget which is lopsided due to mandatory requirements under the heads 'Defence Pensions' and MoD (Civil) besides revenue budget under the head 'Defence Services Estimates' (DSE) that mainly comprises salaries of serving personnel. A slew of measures have been recommended by experts and defence analysts over the last few years to balance the revenue and capital expenditure within the head 'DSE'. It becomes imperative to analyse developments towards modernisation of the armed forces, progress on 'Joint Theatre Commands' in line with leading military powers, especially when CDS is a reality now and finally the restructuring of the Armed Forces that has happened till date.

3.5.1 Defence Budget and Modernisation of the Armed Forces

As per the data released by Global think-tank SIPRI for the year 2021, India is currently the third largest military spender in the world. The top five countries in terms of military expenditure are as under:

Table 2: Top five countries in the world in terms of Defence Expenditure (2021)

Countries	*Spending (In billion US$)*	*% of GDP*
USA	801.0	3.5
China	293.0	1.7
India	**76.6**	**2.15**
UK	68.4	2.2
Russia	65.9	4.1

India's spending has increased by 33% over the last decade. However, its primary adversary China has the defence budget steadily growing for 27 consecutive years since 1994, to be at a stage where it spends four times that of India on defence.

India's larger Defence Budget includes both MoD and MHA, including four Border Guarding Forces (BGFs) i.e., BSF, ITBP, AR and SSB. Focussing on only revenue and capital share in MoD's Budget (FY 22-23), the details as per ORF issue brief are as under:

Table 3: India's Defence Budget (2022-23)

Heads	*Revenue Expenditure (INR Billion)*	*Capital Expenditure (INR Billion)*	*Total (INR Bn)*
MoD (Civil)	120.50	80.50	201.00
Defence Pensions	1196.96	0.00	1196.96
Defence Services	2330.01	1523.70	3853.70
Total	3647.47	1604.20	5251.66
% of Total	69	31	100

Further, delving deep and focussing only on Defence Services, the following table shows the Revenue-Capital Ratio of Armed Forces for FY 2022-23:

Table 4: Revenue-Capital Expenditure Ratio of three services of Indian Armed Forces Defence Budget (2022-23)

Expenditure Head	*Army*	*Navy*	*Air Force*
Revenue Expenditure	1648.98	254.06	328.73
Capital Expenditure	321.35	475.91	568.52
Total (INR Billion)	1970.33	729.97	897.25
Share of Revenue Expenditure (%)	84	35	37
Share of Capital Expenditure (%)	16	65	63

This clearly indicates that Army has only 16% of the allocated budget to spend on modernisation whereas the Navy and Air Force spend approximately almost two-third of their allocated budget on the same. This is directly proportional to the numeric strength of the Indian Army, vis-à-vis the other two services, as a major chunk of budget under Revenue head is spent on salaries of service personnel followed by the maintenance of huge inventory of equipment and services in the Indian Army. Overall, out of a defence budget of approximately ₹ 5.2 Lakh Crores, ₹ 1.6 Lakh Crores are available for modernisation in FY 2022-23 which is 31% of total allocation. This is certainly unhealthy figure for the Armed Forces as they are badly in need of modernisation in all three services. One fact that has come to light in view of reduction in Indian Army's modernisation budget compared to the last financial year is not due to resource crunch, rather Army's inability to spend the allocated budget effectively. The Army needs to learn from the Navy, which has been able to draw 44% more towards modernisation in the present financial year owing to its well planned and timely expenditure in the previous financial year. This must be the priority for Indian Army, as reduced modernisation expenditure amidst the Chinese Military Aggression in Eastern Ladakh is a matter of concern.

It is a paradox that when the Indian Army needs to invest on disruptive technologies like Artificial Intelligence, which will see an increasing role in future warfare over and above acquisitions in the pipeline, they are surrendering funds. A portion of the budget is required to be reserved for investing on such cutting-edge platform that will go a long way in sustaining the military in future.

3.5.2 Organisational Restructuring of the Indian Army

The character of warfare has changed and the present geo-political global scenario warrants that we are prepared for both short, intense and cutting-edge high technology driven wars and long drawn stand-off akin to one in Eastern Ladakh. This calls for a comprehensive strategic review driven National Security Strategy combined with speedy decisions by the new CDS, appointed after over nine months since the tragic and unfortunate death of Gen Bipin Rawat, who set the ball rolling in this direction. The quality and size of the Armed Forces will also be dictated by this, with principal focus on quality over quantity or class over mass. There is a scope to reduce the size as we move towards theaterisation and lot of work has been done. However, much work remains, to make India future combat ready. Towards organisational restructuring of Indian Army, some revolutionary steps taken towards future warfare are highlighted as under:

- A new appointment of Deputy Chief of Army Staff (Strategy) or DCOAS (S) of 'Lieutenant General' (Lt Gen) Rank raised (by subsuming the appointment of Director General Rashtriya Rifles), who has under him Military Operations, Military Intelligence, Operational Logistics and **Information Warfare** Directorates.
- A new appointment of Director General Information Warfare (DGIW) raised (by subsuming the appointment of Director General Military Training (DGMT) of Lt Gen Rank to Army Training Command, ARTRAC). This is an important move keeping in view future warfare, as he becomes responsible for needs of future battlefield, Hybrid Warfare and Social Media realities.
- Erstwhile DCOAS (Planning and Systems) is now christened as DCOAS (Capability Development and Sustenance).
- Erstwhile DG (Weapons & Equipment) is now DG (Capability Development).
- Erstwhile Master General (Ordnance) is now MG (Sustenance).
- Erstwhile DCOAS (Information Systems and Training) is now christened as DCOAS (Information Systems and Coordination).

The restructured organisation of Indian Army is at **Appendix 'A'**.

3.5.3 Progress on India's Joint Theatre Commands

One of the positive developments post recommendations of a Group of Ministers set up by Cabinet Secretary on Security (CSS) following the Kargil Review Committees has been the creation of the post of CDS in December 2019, almost 19 years after the recommendations were submitted on 26 February 2001 to then Prime Minister Atal Bihari Vajpayee. Finally, India joined around 70 countries that have CDS like posts for facilitating integration in military planning and operations among three services. These include all P5 nations, though with different geo-strategic settings, i.e., USA (since 1942), China (since 1948), France (since 1948), UK (since 1959) and Russian Federation (since 1992).

General Bipin Rawat, the first CDS of the Indian Armed Forces, who took over on 01 Jan 2020, was also the permanent Chairman of the

Chiefs of Staff Committee (COSC) and laid the groundwork for "integrated theatre commands", the warfighting entities, containing Army, Navy and Air Force components, for synergy in combat power of all three services. He revealed the shape of India's 'Joint Theatre Commands', for the first time in September 2021, where 17 single-service commands (Army-07, Air Force-07 and Navy-03) at present have been proposed to be subsumed into 4 x Joint Theatre Commands, as under:

- 2x Land-based Commands (one each for Pakistan and China)
- 1x Air Defence Command
- 1x Maritime Command

Over and above, two unified commands, Andaman and Nicobar Command (ANC) as geographical command and Strategic Forces Command (SFC) as functional command responsible for 'Nuclear Capability' are already in place.

Unfortunately, genuine integration among the three services with proposed unified theatre commands remains a work in progress, with the first CDS passing away in a tragic Indian Air Force (IAF) Chopper crash in the Nilgiri Hills in Tamil Nadu on 08 December 2021 and the vacancy filled up, only after a gap of over nine months, thus further pushing back the envisaged timelines for proposed unified theatre commands.

Based on the recommendations of the Naresh Chandra Task Force submitted to the then Prime Minister Dr. Manmohan Singh on 23 May 2012, to create a 'Cyber Command', an 'Aerospace Command' and a 'Special Operations Command', the tri-services based Defence Cyber Agency (DCA), Defence Space Agency (DSA) and the Armed Forces Special Operations Division (AFSOD) were created and made operational in November 2019. All these are likely to be converted into full-sized tri-services functional commands to handle these critical domains as and when theaterisation materialises. The structure has been proposed taking cue from some leading military powers like USA and China.

3.5.4 Way Forward

India, despite spending over 2% of GDP and having third largest defence budget globally, does not get requisite bang for buck. Some of the reasons analysed for this lacuna are:

- Its military imports, accounting for 11% of the total global weapons imported in 2021, is the highest globally and far outweighs its exports, 0.2% of total exports, at 23rd position, keeping it vulnerable strategically.
- Absence of official National Security Strategy has resulted in lack of long-term goals for systematic military capability build-up with inter-services prioritisation.
- Need to balance teeth-to-tail ratio, slashing non-operational flab while keeping adequate ground forces, focussing on quality over quantity.
- Weak domestic industrial base and military-industrial complex.
- Genuine integration among tri-services with unified theatre commands remains to be completed, further jeopardised by vacant CDS post for more than nine months since 09 Dec 2021.

The following are recommended to be monitored by respective stakeholders and completed within the stipulated timelines:

- Drafting of National Security Strategy with inter-se priorities among the services for enhancing military capabilities commensurate to threat perception. Four years have already elapsed since DPC was entrusted with this mandate. It must come out with one without any further delay, duly dovetailing important AI strategies for national security, before the present Government completes its term in May 2024.
- Steps for Aatmanirbhar Bharat in Defence have already been taken by earmarking 68% of the capital procurement budget for domestic industry in FY 2022-23. The same is required to be periodically monitored and a portion earmarked for R&D and innovations in the field of AI.
- Exports and indigenous production targets of $5 billion and

$25 billion by 2025 be kept a track of so as to achieve this target on time.

- Restructuring of armed forces is in progress and some goals have been achieved. However, some proposals are being worked out and refined by the Department of Military Affairs for final decision by the new CDS, appointed on 28 September 2022 after a delay of over nine months. Speculations and "off-the-cuff" remarks on the issue by so called defence analysts that invariably get highlighted by social media are of no consequence except creating controversies and heart burns. For instance, considering reduction of pension bill as a major factor towards restructuring and modernisation of Armed Forces, the policy of short-service commission for officers presently in vogue and short-service engagements for soldiers of at least 10 years, duly covered by a contributory pension scheme and 'veteran' status with all benefits, seems to be the best method to reduce the pension bill. This approach is followed by all advanced military powers and is time-tested. After all, we have realised after Kargil War, the importance of the CDS and Geographical Theatre Commands/Functional Commands, already implemented by all advanced armies such as China, USA and Russia. A new CDS, though appointed after a gap of over nine months, is in order to continue to spearhead doctrinal and transformational changes across various domains at the earliest and ensure future-combat preparedness of Indian Armed Forces. As brought out recently by the CDS General Anil Chauhan, "theaterisation is on the anvil." Recent developments indicate that theatre commands may see the light of the day in the second half of the year 2023.

Till theatre commands come up, the AI efforts by all three services may be synergised and co-ordinated by respective Design Bureaus so as to mutually benefit from each other, avoid re-inventing the wheel and create a pool of talent within the forces to implement use cases with an eye on short-term, mid-term and long-term goals of the three services.

4

India and Artificial Intelligence: Key Initiatives

4.1 INDIA STEPS INTO THE AI ARENA: GOVERNMENT INITIATIVES

On 24 August 2022, India will complete five years since stepping into AI Arena when the Ministry of Commerce and Industry (MoCI), GoI constituted an AI task force of 18 members under the chairmanship of Dr. V Kamakoti, Professor, IIT Madras on Artificial Intelligence for India's Economic Transformation on 24 August 2017. While this was the first step for India to build AI vision, it came at a time when many countries already had AI policies, strategies and time-bound goals in place. Another task force was constituted by DDP under Ministry of Defence (MoD) to explore India's priorities for development of AI in civilian and military spheres on 02 Feb 2018. The 16-member Task Force for "Strategic Implementation of AI for National Security and Defence" was headed by N Chandrasekaran, Chairman Tata Sons. Both the task forces submitted their reports to respective Ministries on 19 June 2018 and 30 Jun 2018 respectively.

Assigning different aims to the two task forces, MoCI task force and MoD task force brings to the fore, India's traditional tendency to keep civilian and military challenges separately. However, in the hindsight, it seems to be a wise step, given the scenario that India is a late starter on AI adoption and in absence of any ground work on various related issues, such as talent pool, state of expertise in private and public sector, R&D facilities, infrastructure, identification of use cases for civilian and military applications of AI and Global Strategic Partnerships, the think-tanks with the best of talents from a variety of fields were required to come up with recommendations on both aspects of AI use, i.e., for solving socio-economic problems leading to economic transformation of Indian Society and strategic implications from National Security perspective.

Based on the recommendation for the MoD task force, the DDP, GoI issued a government order on 08 Feb 2019 (original document attached as **Appendix 'B'**). The salient points of this order, now implemented, are as under:

- A high level 'Defence AI Council' (DAIC) established under chairmanship of Honourable Raksha Mantri and to convene at least twice a year for speedy adoption of AI.
- A Defence AI Projects Agency (DAIPA) formed with Secretary (Defence Production) as the ex-officio head, allocated ₹ 100 Crores by MoD each year for next five years for implementation of AI related recommendations of Task Force.
- Earmarking of ₹ 100 Crores each year for next five years by each Service Headquarters (SHQs) from their annual budgetary allocations, for AI specific application development.
- AI training of defence personnel, courses in all defence training centres and institutes to create AI specialists within forces.
- Capacity building within defence and integration of AI into India's Defence Strategy.

4.2 RECOMMENDATIONS OF THE AI TASK FORCES

The vision that formed the basis of report and recommendations of the MoCI Task Force considers AI to be used by the Government as a socio-economic problem solver rather than just boosting economic growth. The report considers three issues to be addressed, firstly, the areas for Government's role; secondly the ways AI can improve life and solve problems of Indian citizens and thirdly identifying sectors that can generate employment and growth using AI Technology. 'National Security' is one of the 10 domains specifically identified for AI use.

However, the report has minimally engaged with the ethical concerns by use of AI under this domain, while indicating some of the areas for its use and deployment, such as Autonomous Surveillance and Combat Systems, Adaptive Communication Systems, AI based cyber-attack mitigation and counter-attack systems and multi-sensor data fusion based on decision-making systems. Deploying these systems is a huge challenge in terms of cost, technology availability and system management capability deficit.

For enabling the correct implementation and adoption of projects relevant to each domain, Ministries and Departments of GoI have been mapped. In case of 'National Security', relevant to this research work, the report recommends Ministries of Atomic Energy, Defence, Electronics and IT, External Affairs, Home Ministry, Power, Railways, Road Transport and Highways, Shipping and Space and, National Security Council Secretariat. The report recommends creation of consortium of Micro, Small and Medium Enterprises (MSMEs) for development of autonomous systems, protecting digital data from external cyber threats by development methodologies and integration of infrastructure existing for provisioning need based real-time information through AI-based techniques embedded in the platform, to security agencies for threat mitigation.

The eight key recommendations of the report include 'National Artificial Intelligence Mission (N-AIM)' to be funded by Union Budget Nodal Agency for five years totalling ₹ 1200 Crores (₹ 240 Crores per year) for coordinating AI activities; Setting up digital data bank, for cross-industry data and information; Enabling policies; International Norms on AI-based technologies, Human Resource Development; Re-skilling; International Rule Making and Bilateral Cooperation.

The MoD task force, after meetings held, felt the need to list down 'Use Cases' for AI development in various functional areas. For civilian use the functional areas identified were personnel, supply chain and logistics, predictive maintenance and finance & accounting. For military areas, functional areas constituted were Lethal Autonomous Weapon Systems (LAWS), Unmanned Surveillance and Simulated War Game & Training. For dual use, Cybersecurity, Aerospace Security and

Intelligence & Reconnaissance were identified. However, some more functional areas for military use could have been identified so as to not lose sight of them and set the goals in correct perspective even though achievable in long-term. To compensate for this initial oversight, Army Design Bureau (ADB) has set the ball rolling in identifying terrain-specific user requirements.

4.3 NITI AAYOG'S INITIATIVE IN AI

'The National Institution for Transforming India' or NITI Aayog in short, is the premier policy think-tank of GoI providing directorial and policy inputs. It came into being on 01 January 2015 replacing Planning Commission. Recognising AI's potential to transform economies across the globe and the need for India to strategise its approach, NITI Aayog was mandated to establish the National Program on AI.

Following the recommendations of the task force and prioritising the role of Government to evolve the national strategy for AI which is also one of the crucial parameters set towards Global AI Readiness, they have published the strategy document in a time-bound manner, to be among the top 25 countries that have achieved this goal. The document is based on the premise that India has the potential to be among leaders on the global AI map—with a unique brand **#AI for All**.

4.3.1 Discussion Paper on National Strategy for AI (NSAI)

The objectives drawn from the "National Strategy for AI" are as under:

- **The Economic Impact of AI for India**. AI has the potential to drive economic growth through enabling:
  - Intelligent Automation
  - Labour & Capital Augmentation
  - Innovations

New goods, services and innovations enabled via AI will create economic value.

- **AI for Social Development and Inclusive Growth**

  AI being a disruptive technology will have transformative

impact for improving the quality of life and access of choice to a larger section of the country. Agriculture, healthcare, inclusive financial growth, smart cities and infrastructure sectors have unique challenges that will be effectively solved by AI.

- **AI Garage for 40% of the World**

  The AI strategy envisages India to be the "AI Garage" for developing and emerging economies, where institutions and enterprises develop scalable solutions, thereby providing solutions for 40% of developing economies or even more. Thus, India is projected as the most appropriate destination for R&D and innovation in the field of AI.

- **Focus Areas**

  The strategy document has prioritised five sectors to focus on for AI intervention that will help solve the societal problems. These are as under:

  - **Healthcare.** To increase access and affordability of quality healthcare.
  - **Agriculture.** To increase profitability and reduction of wastage, thus enhancing income of farmers.
  - **Education**. Improved access and quality of education across a wider population.
  - **Smart Cities & Infrastructure**. AI can augment the features of smart cities such as smart parks and public facilities, smart homes, crowd management, intelligent safety systems and remedial measures for cyber attacks to cater for burgeoning urban population.
  - **Smart Mobility & Transportation.** AI can be employed for safer modes of transportation and managing congestion-free traffic movements and reduced accidents.

Out of 10 domains recommended by the MoCI Task Force, five priority domains have been focussed on for AI intervention in the NSAI. Significantly, 'National Security' domain has been left out in the strategy document. However, this may have been done owing to the MoD Task Force having been mandated to study the same. The importance of AI in future warfare has been highlighted by the Indian Prime Minister as well as then Chief of the Army Staff (COAS) and later CDS Late Gen Bipin Rawat in 2018. This was reiterated by the Hon'ble Raksha Mantri, Shri Rajnath Singh who, while launching 75 newly developed defence AI products and technologies on the eve of 75 years of India's Independence during an event in New Delhi on 11 Jul 2022, stated: "We must develop the capability of our AI technology so that no country can even think of ruling us." India has actively participated in convention for Certain Conventional Weapons (CCW) and emphasised that the risks to strategic stability owing to development of LAWS needs to be looked into. India considers responsible military use of AI as necessary believing that 'human control' needs to be ensured and weaponised platforms cannot be given complete autonomy.

Following tasks have been envisaged for the Government to implement in its role as facilitator and promoter of AI:

- Promoting AI Research and Application by setting up Centres of Research Excellence (CORE) for AI and International Centres for Transformational AI (ICTAI).
- Establishing a 'Common Data Computing Platform' for Big Data Analytics with large AI computing infrastructure connecting all COREs, ICTAIs and other academic institutions such as 'AIRAWAT', acronym for '**AI** **R**esearch, **A**nalytics and kno**W**ledge **A**ssimilation pla**T**form'.
- Creating a CERN for AI by bringing together other interested national governments.
- Re-skilling and Training. Investment in re-skilling and training should be incentivised by the Government through tax-breaks and grants.
- Development of Human Resources. Government needs to introduce AI/ML teaching from school level and build skilled AI workforce.

4.3.2 Principles for Responsible AI

The release of the AI strategy discussion paper earlier in June 2018 was a stepping stone towards rolling out of an ambitious programme that would ensure use of responsible AI both in civil and military environment. In February 2021, NITI Aayog came out with the first part of the strategy titled: "Responsible AI #AI for All", an approach paper in collaboration with World Economic Forum Centre for Industry 4.0. The first part covers the "Principles for Responsible AI" to address the AI ethics and governance that is evolving contiguous to the rapidly advancing AI technology. The ethical considerations in this report have been divided into two broad categories, i.e., "System Considerations" and "Societal Considerations". The former encompasses those arising due to system design choices and deployment processes such as inherent bias, potential exclusion, accountability assignment, privacy and security risks and the latter includes impact on jobs and malicious psychological profiling.

Based on the principle ensuring that AI systems are designed so as to enable fundamental rights, the following principles, derived from the tenets of Indian Constitution have been recommended for responsible management of AI systems and serve as the guiding framework for various stakeholders in leveraging AI:

Principles of Safety and Reliability.

- Principle of Equality.
- Principles of Inclusivity and Non-Discrimination.
- Principles of Protection and Reinforcement of Positive Human Values.
- Principle of Transparency.
- Principle of Accountability.
- Principle of Privacy and Security.

4.3.3 Operationalisation of Principles for Responsible AI

Addressing ethics and privacy issues from the use of AI is the step that will address most of the concerns of the citizens of a democratic set up. It is being addressed across the world, along with regulatory mechanisms that need to be put in place to solve this issue.

Honourable Prime Minister Shri Narendra Modi has also stressed upon importance of ensuring responsible use of technology at the Davos meet in Jan 2021. NITI Aayog has now laid the groundwork for operationalising the 'Principles towards Responsible Use of AI' that it earlier released as Part I. The approach document forms Part II of the strategy, released in August 2021 and titled 'Operationalising Principles for Responsible AI'. The operationalisation and adoption of the principles in the AI ecosystem in India will lead to maximisation of benefits of AI for all while minimising AI-related risks. The actions to be adopted in order to drive responsible AI are divided among three stakeholders: The Government, The Private Sector and Research Institutions tasked as under:

- **The Government**. Designing ideal regulatory and policy interventions, creating awareness, accessibility and capacity building and facilitating precise procurement strategies.
- **The Private Sector**. Incentivising ethics by design, creating frameworks for compliance with relevant AI standards and guidelines. This is a necessity as there are 3465 start-ups focussed on AI in India (as per online encyclopaedia Tracxn) as on date.
- **Research Institutions.** Promoting responsible AI practices in research. Such mechanisms can start by introducing ethical reasoning in the curriculum.

A 'Council for Ethics and Technology' (CET) as the advisory body to guide responsible AI ecosystem is proposed for India to include 'National Security Expert' as a member among other members.

The Stanford AI index report shows that India has the highest AI skill penetration rate in the world. Hence, building a robust AI Ecosystem is crucial for India as it aspires to establish itself as a hub for AI development.

4.4 AI ACCELERATORS AND ENABLERS

Artificial Intelligence technology is heavily dependent on enabling technologies, such as robust cloud platform for Big Data Analytics and assimilation, semiconductor chips with higher power efficiency and high throughput processing super computing systems with petaFLOPS/

exaFLOPS computing infrastructure. These enablers can further AI's potential for another 10-15 years with better and improved machine learning algorithms. From India's perspective, a giant step has already been taken towards improvement on all three fronts—a ₹ 7000 Crore budget sanction for AIRAWAT to support advancement of AI-based developments in 2019, over a period of five years, a US$ 10 billion package for indigenous semiconductor ecosystem as also joining hands with QUAD members on security resilient semiconductor supply chain in 2021, and a ₹ 4500 Crore National Supercomputing Mission (NSM) in 2015, spread over a period of seven years, aimed to connect R&D institutions and academic institutions. These three accelerators of AI are analysed below.

4.4.1 AIRAWAT: The Common Compute Platform

The Common Compute Platform—'AIRAWAT' is an acronym for **AI** **R**esearch, **A**nalytics and Kno**w**ledge **A**ssimilation Pla**t**form which has been recommended in the NSAI document by NITI Aayog. The Government role is envisaged to set up a common cloud platform for Big Data Analytics and Assimilation with a large, power optimised AI Computing Infrastructure connecting all COREs, ICTAIs and other academic institutions with National Knowledge Network (NKN). This approach will reduce infrastructural requirements due to pooling efficiencies and reduce operational and maintenance costs. While keeping national data secure, AIRAWAT will support advancements of AI-based developments in Image Recognition, Speech Recognition and NLP for research as also advancements in Agriculture, Healthcare and Education.

The AI computing infrastructure is proposed to be set up on similarities as Japan's ABCI (AI Bridging Cloud Infrastructure) AI Supercomputing Facility. NITI Aayog had requested the Government to invest ₹ 7500 Crores initially over a three-year period. However, the expenditure finance committee (Ministry of Finance) has cleared ₹ 7000 Crores over a five-year period to be spent till 2024-25. A high-level task force as requested by NITI Aayog to oversee its roll-out and implementation is also being set up.

4.4.2 Resilient Semiconductor Chain

Emerging technology like AI among other technologies like 5G cannot flourish without a viable semiconductor industry. As India has joined the AI arena, the lack of semiconductor ecosystem in the country will certainly hurt its prospects towards positioning itself among the leading adopters of the technology globally. The cabinet approval of US$ 10 billion incentive package to create local semiconductor industry is a welcome step. It will reduce the imports drastically and alter its image for the better on world scene. However, India should be cautiously building on the expertise already available locally, and that is to become original manufacturer for low-cost medium and low-end chips of order of 20 nanometres, and not high end and advanced chips of order of 3-5 nanometres as India can ill-afford the loss if the investment fails, as the infrastructure cost runs into several billion dollars annually. Secondly, India having low-cost skilled technical 'manpower', can make its presence felt in assembly, testing and packaging (ATP) segment, where at the moment, China leads.

Further, the QUAD alliance met in September 2021 to strengthen and secure the global semiconductor supply chain in order to contain China in this strategic sector. QUAD members observed that resilient, secure and diverse semiconductor supply chains are vital to shared national interests and can reduce the dependency on adversaries by leveraging their combined capabilities to advance semiconductor innovation and enhance supply chain resiliency. The first-ever summit of QUAD leaders and the agreement has taken place at a crucial time when there is a global shortage of semiconductors. Multilateral cooperation on semiconductors is the way forward for India, which has fallen short in self-sufficiency on semiconductor front. Globally, Taiwan is the leading semiconductor manufacturer producing over half of the world's semiconductor requirements, especially advanced chips up to 5 nanometres. Taiwan Semiconductor Manufacturing Company (TSMC) plans to put 3 nanometres FinFET chips into volume production by the second half of 2022. 3 nanometres chips will reduce power consumption by 25% at the same-speed, increase speed by 10-15% at the same power and increase transistor density by about 33%, compared to the 5 nanometres FinFET chips.

As the AI revolution surges, and weaponised AI dominance becomes the parameter for defining global leaders in cutting edge technology, USA and China are vying for top spot in the AI capability race. The QUAD's focus to secure and strengthen semiconductor chain is also owing to global dependency on Taiwan which has strained ties with China. The recent Chinese forays violating Taiwanese Air Space, and such other nefarious activities may lead to supply chain getting disrupted, if the situation escalates. QUAD, with its synergised capabilities in this area must develop a self-reliant resilient chain within a framework that is vital for technology design and development, and governance and use, so as to eliminate the possibility of any sort of interference from the adversary.

4.4.3 National Supercomputing Mission

One of the important indicators indicative of a country's good technological infrastructure supporting AI Technologies is the number of supercomputers it has, especially in Top 500 Supercomputer List.

India at present has just three supercomputers in the top 500 list and none of them in top 100 supercomputers in terms of computing power as per the 50th edition of Top 500 list released on 01 Jun 2022. The National Supercomputing Mission (NSM) launched in 2015 with an investment of ₹ 4500 Crores has the potential to propel India into top 10 nations in terms of combined computing power. This will empower researchers and scientists to conduct cutting-edge research in AI and other domains. The mission guided jointly by Ministry of Electronics & IT (MeitY) and Department of Science & Technology (DST) has entrusted the task of overall design, development, deployment and commissioning of supercomputers with Centre for Development of Advanced Computing (C-DAC). Out of three phases planned under NSM, Phase 1 focussed on ecosystem for assembly of system components indigenously. Phase 2 that started in April 2021 aimed to manufacture supercomputers with an indigenous software stack in the country. Phase 3, also initiated in 2021 focusses on design and manufacturing in the country. Phase 1 and 2 aims to install 15 systems with total computing power of 22 petaFLOPS in premier research institutions. PARAM Siddhi-AI, the fastest supercomputer of

India has been built under NSM. Phase 3 will expectedly take total computing speed to 50 petaFLOPS, with the plan to install three systems of 3 petaFLOPS each and one system with 20 petaFLOPS at the national facility. All three phases will facilitate around 75 top institutions of India, an access to High Performance Computing (HPC) connected through National Knowledge Network (NKN).

The NSM is a seven-year mission (2015-2022) due to be completed by 2022 end. It should not miss the deadline of December 2022 as far as completion of Phase 3 is concerned, because it is this ambitious phase of the mission that may steer India among top 10 nations in global rankings in terms of total number of supercomputers (expected to be a total of eight of them in top 500 list) and total computing power of 50-60 petaFLOPS in the next edition of the Top 500 list, likely in November 2022/June 2023.

4.5 LEVERAGING AI IN DEFENCE APPLICATIONS

MoD initiated the process of preparing Indian defence forces for use of AI. A multi-stakeholder Task Force formed by members from the Government, Defence Services, Academia, Industry, DRDO, Defence Public Sector Undertakings (DPSUs), National Cyber Security Coordinator, Indian Space and Research Organisation (ISRO), Bhabha Atomic Research Centre (BARC) and start-ups was constituted to study the issues on the implications of AI on National Security and Defence needs in February 2018. The following pointers emerged from the study:

- Roadmap outlined for AI adoption in the defence sector and integrating and embedding AI strategy with core defence strategy.
- DPSUs and Ordnance Factories were assigned a roadmap for developing AI enabled products.
- DRDO was assigned projects and funds allocated on case-to-case basis.
- AI-based tools were aimed to assist defence personnel in supporting operations, maintenance and logistics.

4.5.1 DRDO and DPSU Initiatives in AI Field

For application-oriented research in AI, two DRDO labs, both based in Bengaluru, are specialised laboratories on the job. The first one is Centre for Artificial Intelligence and Robotics (CAIR), established in October 1986 with research focus in the areas of AI, Robotics, Logistics and Control Systems and Information & Communication Technology (ICT), addressing emerging requirements in Information, AI and Robotics domains of 5GW. The last of the five goals of this core AI laboratory of DRDO is worth mentioning: 'Driving the national debate where technology policy is critical to preserving national security and self-sufficiency'.

The second one is DRDO Young Scientist Laboratory–AI (DYSL-AI) established on 02 June 2020, one of the five specialised research laboratories dealing with a focussed area of science. As per the norms laid out, everyone, including Director, at the lab is under 35 years of age, to enable engage young talent in India with leadership abilities in cutting-edge and challenging technologies. Besides these two, all DRDO System Laboratories, having AI technological groups are capable of incorporating AI features into products under development as confirmed during an interaction with the DRDO chairman Dr. G Satheesh Reddy on his visit to Savitribai Phule Pune University on 27 August 2021.

Besides nine Defence PSUs already existing, seven more DPSUs were carved out w.e.f. 01 October 2021 covering all 41 Ordnance Factories under administrative control of Ordnance Factory Board earlier, as part of restructuring plan to unleash new growth potential and innovation while ensuring enhancement of functional autonomy. Central Government with single focus on emerging technologies has made it mandatory for DPSU, to initiate projects in AI. DPSUs have already collaborated with DRDO to implement projects on AI that would aid the armed forces constructively in areas such as decision support, sensor data analysis, security, predictive maintenance, situational awareness, accurate data extraction etc. Some of them are as tabulated below:

Table 5: AI Projects through collaboration between DRDO and DPSUs

Name of the Project	*Purpose*	*Agency*	*Budget*
1. **AI-Based solutions for Signal Intelligence; Jan 2019**	Enhance intelligence, collation and analysis of capabilities for the armed forces	CAIR (DRDO)	₹ 73.9 Crores
2. **Energy Harvesting-based Infrared Sensor Network for Automated Human Intrusion Detection (EYESIRa); Jan 2019**	Powered by AI & IoT for detecting human intrusion on borders by Armed Forces	CAIR (DRDO) Status: CONFIDENTIAL	₹ 1.8 Crores
3. **First Responder Robot; Dec 2018**	Security of Indian Borders	BEL (DPSU) in collaboration with CRL	BEL to invest ₹ 40-50 Crores per annum for next three years (2019-2022).
4. **Establishment of AI Centre at MCTE, Mhow (Indian Army Category 'A' establishment)**	For research and training in AI with deployments in forward areas.	Active support of industry and academia.	-
5. **RUSTOM 2 UAV (Medium Altitude Long Endurance (MALE) UAV); February 2018**	Developed on the lines of predator drones of the US to carry out surveillance and reconnaissance (ISR) roles for the Armed forces.	Aeronautical Development Establishment (ADE), DRDO, HAL and BEL	₹ 1500 Crores
6. **QNu Labs—Indian Army, AI Research Centre, EM Spectrum and National Security and Cyber Warfare; October 2019.**	Impetus in Indian Army's technological institutions for investing in AI, Cyber-security and Quantum.	Quantum Computing Labs MCTE (Research & Training)	-

DPSUs have been asked by the MoD to invest in tapping potential business in the area of AI. Currently, BEL with an investment of ₹ 150 Crores over three years, is working on five major AI projects which include the following:

- Facial recognition for security applications.
- IoT based platform maintenance.
- Social networking analysis.

- Robotics surveillance platform.
- Automated Information extraction and synthesis.

4.5.2 Army Design Bureau and AI Use Cases

The Indian Army's 'Make in India' initiative is spearheaded by the Army Design Bureau (ADB) which is in-charge of creating an effective interface with the defence industry and the academia for development of futuristic systems. It is headed by an Additional Director General (Major General) directly under the aegis of Deputy Chief of Army Staff (Capability Development and Sustenance).

Its charter is to drive the employment of AI for defence needs and identify appropriate technology/ equipment and weapons system for offensive and defensive operations including logistics management and training. The AI projects are being progressed under the co-development process via Make-II, Technology Development Fund (TDF), Army Technological Board (ATB), Innovations for Defence Excellence (iDEX) and Defence Innovation Organisation (DIO) routes.

AI Use cases for Indian Army. In the last 4-5 years, ADB has catalysed innovations and created institutionalised mechanisms to mentor and support the defence industry and academia to facilitate technological ascendancy. An interaction with ADB has led to latest updates on problem definition statements that have been compiled to seek tailor-made solutions to the felt-requirement of the Indian Army. Out of 150 problem definition statements so identified, some of the projects are in progress through Make-II, TDF, iDEX or ATB route, some are being progressed through DRDO and DIO route, some fully matured products are being pursued through Direct Commercial Sales (DCS) route and balance are live use cases, solutions for which are being sought. Some of the AI use cases under specific AI domains with project status are enumerated below:

Table 6: AI Projects under progress through ADB

AI: USE CASES	
Lethal Autonomous Weapons	
1. **Swarming of Remotely Piloted Aircraft**	Under progress.
Autonomous Weapons	
2. **AI-IED / Mine Detection**	Under progress (through ATB).
Intelligence, Surveillance and Reconnaissance	
3. **Data Analysis: VYOMA**—Collating and analysing intelligence out of intelligence summary and reports.	Under progress.
4. **Border/Perimeter Defence:** • AI monitor for surveillance • Smartisation of Anti-Infiltration Obstacle System (**AIOS**)	Live Status; Solutions being sought as per ADB Compendium 2020.
5. **Object and Pattern Recognition:** • Image Analysis • Face Recognition	Under progress.
6. **Speech/Language Translation:** • Mandarin to English translation • NLP (Speech Recognition)	Under progress.
Supply Chain and Logistics	
7. **AI in Inventory Management**	Solutions being sought.
8. **Robotic Mule (with defined Payload)**	
9. **Logistics Management System (KRIDA)**	Under progress.
Personnel: Medical & Healthcare	
10. **Predictive Analysis of Health Data**	Under progress.
11. **Cancer Detection**	
Training	
12. **3-D Modelling of Border Areas**	Under progress.

4.5.3 Army NFS Cloud System for Defence Applications

A highly encrypted cloud system of the Indian Army, similar to NIC's Megh Raj to store personnel as well as operational data, was inaugurated by then Defence Minister Late Manohar Parrikar on 08 November, 2015 in line with the forces' plan to be a "Digital Army".

The "Army Cloud" under the aegis of Project 'Network for Spectrum' (NFS) includes a central data centre, a near line data centre, both in Delhi and a disaster recovery site for a replication of its critical data along with virtualised servers and data storage in an environmentally controlled complex. This will provide IT infrastructure, including servers for computing, storage, network security equipment centrally for automation of Indian Army. However, the system has been under development to guard against security breaches through hacks that may potentially compromise critical information regarding force deployment, operational plans and command & control nodes.

After some considerable delay owing to many other components being part of the tri-services pan-India turnkey project NFS as also requirement to enhance the NFS budget, the project is nearing completion and expected to be dedicated to the nation by 2023 end. With rolling out of NFS, the Indian Army is set to expand its data centres for the cloud computing network, to secure them from physical and cyberspace attacks. The development is part of Army's move to build its automation capabilities and, store and share data on operations and soldiers over the Army Cloud. Two broad heads for developing applications so as to manage operational and personnel information are Operational Information System (OIS) and Management Information System (MIS) respectively.

NFS will provide more than adequate bandwidth to upload heavy data such as videos, so that ground forces, in need of automation the most, can make use of it.

Once integration with other services is completed, a comprehensive Recognised Air Space Picture (RASP) will be generated to facilitate Air Defence operations.

5

Comparative Study: P5 Nations (China, France, Russia, UK, USA) and India in Context of Artificial Intelligence Strategy, Readiness and Use in Military Applications

> *"Artificial Intelligence is the future, not only for Russia, but for all humankind. Whoever becomes the leader in this sphere will become the ruler of the world."*
>
> —**Vladimir Vladimirovich Putin, Russian President**

5.1 OVERVIEW OF AI STRATEGIES: P5 NATIONS AND INDIA

United States of America, China, United Kingdom, France and Russia form part of five permanent members of the UN Security Council (UNSC), also called P5 Nations. Significantly, at present, India is one of the 10 elected non-permanent members of the UNSC for the two-year tenure till December 2022. Interestingly, Canada not a part of P5, published the world's first National AI Strategy in 2017. Since then, more than 45 other countries have published similar documents as of December 2021 and around 15 countries have confirmed they are drafting one. However, 100 countries are yet to start the process, keeping in view, 160 countries qualify to be considered for ranking in the latest AI readiness index published.

Among the P5 nations, China was the first country to publish AI strategy in 2017, France and United Kingdom in 2018, followed by Russia and United States in 2019. India published the National AI strategy in June 2018. AI strategy of a nation is the guiding document to foster the development of AI. The salient points of AI strategies for all P5 Nations and India are highlighted below in the order they were published in public domain.

- ***China (2017)***

On 20 July 2017 the People's Republic of China released their AI strategy, **'A Next Generation Artificial Intelligence Development Plan'**, one of the most comprehensive in the world. It focusses on R&D and talent development through education and acquisition of skills, as well as implications of ethical norms on National Security. The goals are divided into three parts bound by specific timelines, bringing AI industry at par with competitors by 2020, leading in specific fields such as UAVs, voice and image recognition among others by 2025 and leading completely by 2030 and becoming major AI "innovation centre of the world" by then.

Recently, China has dramatically enhanced its AI infrastructure such as ranking first in having the greatest number of supercomputers in Top 500 list and proliferating 5G infrastructure. Also, it competes with the closest competitor USA in R&D, number of research papers published and hosting an AI hectocorn, ByteDance.

- ***France (2018)***

On 29 March 2018, a conglomerate of French Ministries such as higher education, research and innovation, economy and finance, and Armed Forces published the French strategy for AI titled **'AI For Humanity: French Strategy for AI'**.

The strategy focusses on developing an aggressive data policy for big data, with application of AI on four key strategic sectors, namely healthcare, environment, transport and defence. Funds amount to the tune of € 1.5 billion (US$ 1.8 billions) up to 2022. The coordination and report on annual progress is entrusted with the French National Research Institute for Digital Sciences.

- ***United Kingdom (2018)***

In 2018, Office for Artificial Intelligence published the UK Strategy for AI titled **'Industrial Strategy: AI Sector Deal'**.

The UK Strategy focusses on a business-academia-government partnership identifying six foundations for a successful strategy. These are (i) being world's most innovative economy, (ii) creating jobs, (iii) enabling better earnings, (iv) infrastructure enhancement, (v) ease of doing business, and (vi) raising prosperous communities across the entire country. Funds sanctioned amount to GBP 950 million (US$ 1.3 billion as in December 2020).

Recently in November 2020, the government announced a defence spending of GBP 16.5 billion (US$ 21.8 billion) over four years, to be spent on AI technologies having the potential to revolutionise warfare.

- ***United States of America (February 2019)***

On 11 February 2019, then President Donald J Trump launched the American AI initiative, the Nation's Strategy for promoting American leadership in AI. It prioritised the need to invest in R&D, and ensure safe development, testing and deployment of AI technologies. The White House also stressed on developing an AI-ready workforce and collaboration with foreign partners while promoting U.S. leadership in AI.

As far as funding is concerned, it is unclear as regards Government's investment in AI. The Pentagon spent approximately US$ 7.4 billion on AI in its 2017 budget, as per an article by Tim Dutton, an AI policy researcher based in Canada. Significantly, the growth in R&D for AI has been phenomenal since 2015, and it may likely be due to military and defence agency AI efforts.

The US government released its first annual report in February 2020 followed by guidelines in November 2020 for federal agencies to regulate AI applications in the private sector, to include principles governing AI innovation and growth and build public trust and confidence in AI technologies. The National Defence Authorisation Act (NDAA) for Fiscal Year 2021 directed to coordinate AI research and policy across the federal government.

- ***Russia (October 2019)***

On 10 October 2019, Ministry of Digital Development, Communications and Mass Media, Government of the Russian Federation published the '**National Strategy for the Development of AI**'.

Russia backed by Russian President Vladimir Putin's intent to pursue AI technologies, stating 'Whoever becomes the leader in this field will rule the world', has strongly emphasised on its national interests in the AI strategy that lay down guidelines for developing an "Information Society" by 2030. The guidelines include a National Technology Initiative, Departmental Projects for Federal Executive Bodies and Digital Economy Programs designed to implement the AI framework across sectors. There has been no clarity on funding.

Recently, in December 2020, Russian President presented four ideas for AI policies in AI Journey Conference—establishing experimental legal frameworks for the use of AI, developing practical measures to introduce AI algorithms, providing developers of neural networks with access to big data and boosting domestic AI industries with private investment.

- ***India (June 2018)***

India formally stepped into the AI arena in June 2018, when the apex think-tank of the Government of India, National Institution for Transforming India (NITI Aayog) published the discussion paper on AI strategy titled **'National Strategy on Artificial Intelligence: #AIforAll'**. The Indian strategy focusses on economic growth and leveraging AI to enhance social inclusion. The strategy emphasises on research to address issues of concern related to AI, i.e., ethics, bias and privacy issues. Five sectors have been chosen as key to development of AI for economic growth. These are agriculture, healthcare, education, smart cities & infrastructure and smart transportation & smart mobility.

Funding by the government amounts to ₹ 7000 Crores (USD 949 Million). In 2019, the Ministry of Electronics and Information Technology (MeitY) allocated ₹ 400 Crores for a national AI program. Meanwhile, NITI Aayog has also published approach documents on 'Principles of Responsible AI' and their 'operationalisation'.

All P5 nations as well as India have predominantly focussed on leveraging benefits of AI for society and economic growth. The safe development and deployment of AI-based systems and regulatory mechanisms to address ethical and privacy concerns by its use are being discussed. The sustained AI summer continues and as AI development progresses, there will be an inflection point wherein development and use of lethal autonomous weapons and autonomy within a robust regulatory framework possibly in place by then, will decide the hegemony of a nation. However, no nation will be willing to wait for laws and regulations to be in place, before developing the potential that holds the key, both for the technological edge and national security.

5.2 AN OVERVIEW OF AI READINESS INDEX 2021: P5 NATIONS AND INDIA

AI research and development has been scaling new heights on a regular basis till date since third sustained 'AI Spring' began in 1994. Governments across the world are looking up to AI, having great potential to disrupt the world, in order to gain economic and strategic heft.

A very comprehensive and well-researched report by Oxford Insights has been published in January 2022, gauging global AI readiness through a scientifically assisted methodology and giving an insight into governments' readiness to implement AI in the delivery of public services to their citizens.

The Global AI Readiness Index 2021, which is the fourth edition released on 21 January 2022, measures 42 indicators under 10 dimensions across three pillars within the framework to rank the countries across the world. 160 countries with values for more than 50% of indicators are included in the final list. The three pillars with 10 dimensions across them are as under:

- Government Pillar
- Technology Sector Pillar
- Data & Infrastructure Pillar

To have a more comprehensive and robust picture of government AI index in 2021, four additional indicators were added which are as under:

- Number of AI unicorns
- Number of Research Papers published in AI
- Git Hub commits (indicators of the AI skills present within a population) per 1000 population
- Number of Top 500 supercomputers

USA has the largest number of 'AI Unicorns'. The total number of AI unicorns hosted by USA and China is 52, approximately three times more than the rest of the world. China tops the number of 'research papers' published in AI as also the number of times an academic article on AI is cited. China tops the list yet again with highest number of supercomputers in 'Top 500' list released on 01 June 2022.

Despite five East-Asian countries in top 20 ranked countries in the world, it is one of the most unequal regions in terms of AI readiness. The low scoring countries of East Asia are a disadvantaged due to absence of national AI strategies, lack of data availability compared to their regional peers, and having comparably smaller technology sectors.

Western Europe having a pool of 20 countries has 10 of them in the top 20 ranked countries. Cross-border approach to AI readiness taken within the region is attributed to its growth. Moreover, Nordic countries rank highly in the index despite none of them being large economies. This demonstrates how a country's economic heft does not determine its ranking in the index. It is because of their government's ability to combine institutional strength with business environments that allow for innovation as analysed by experts.

The following table gives the comparative overall rankings, overall score and separate scores across all the three pillars of methodology for P5 nations and India:

Table 7: Global AI Readiness Index 2021 Ranking of P5 Nations and India

Country	*GlobalPosition*		*Overall Score*	*Government*	*Technology Sector*	*Data & Infra-structure*
	2021	2020				
1. USA	1	1	88.16	88.46	83.31	92.71
2. UK	3	2	81.25	85.69	67.26	90.81
3. France	11	11	76.41	82.10	60.61	86.53
4. China	15	19	74.42	83.79	61.33	78.15
5. Russia	38	33	61.93	67.44	46.46	71.90
6. India	51	40	56.11	73.26	48.04	**47.02**

While USA and France maintain their respective global positions since last AI Readiness Index in 2020, UK and Russia have dropped one place and five places respectively. China with a robust AI strategy in 2017 setting out crystal clear goals and milestones to achieve in 2020, 2025 and 2030 are on the rise having gone up by four places, despite geo-political turmoil and COVID-19 stretching up to 2021. UK lost one place at the cost of Singapore which also gained four places, from 6th to 2nd rank owing to high scores in the Data and Infrastructure Pillar, partly due to strong 5G infrastructure and high societal adoption of mobile technologies in the country. Russia has dropped five places and may further drop in rankings next year due to the lengthy nature of so-called Russian Special Military Operations in Ukraine, leading to stringent sanctions imposed and dearth of funds to invest in AI for at least 2-3 years as envisaged. Tremendous resolve and will power will be required by President Putin to match his vision on AI, so as to enable Russia to continue to move up the ranking ladder in coming years. There is certainly a huge gap building up between the other four of the P5 nations and Russia as can be seen from the overall score and rankings of the AI index 2021. India will certainly challenge Russia over next 2-3 years in AI domain, provided it improves the data and infrastructure score, proving to be stumbling block for this emerging power.

China seems all set to overtake France and UK and even challenge USA on at least one of the three AI development pillars mentioned above by the year 2025, as seen by its aggressive approach towards AI development, backed by a sound AI strategy and development plan, despite all odds.

Finally, India ranked 51st having dropped 11 places from its previous 40th rank in 2020, has a lot of catching up to do with the P5 Nations and the time is now. They cannot afford to miss the deadline, especially when they aspire to be a US$5 trillion economy and third largest economic superpower by 2030. Government has taken the initiative to go up the ranking ladder in coming years, bettering at least one of the P5 Nations, Russia on this pillar. India is ranked higher than Russia even on the technology sector pillar. However, their low overall ranking mainly attributes to their dismal global ranking on 'data and infrastructure' pillar which leaves India at a lowly 111th out of 160 countries, pulling it down on overall global ranking. India has the potential to break into top 25 nations on AI Readiness within 2-3 years if the investments that have been made in developing the infrastructure, data availability and data representation, bear fruits within stipulated timelines and without any hiccups. The key areas are 5G infrastructures, number of supercomputers and cloud computing platforms, internet access and minimising gender gap in internet and mobile access. To augment the cause through technology pillar, where India is already ranked 30th globally, number of AI and non-AI unicorns, computer software spending, R&D spending, research papers published in AI, digital skills and quality of engineering and technology higher education will be the key as government has initiated mechanisms to improve all these indicators. Finally, the already healthy-looking government pillar, may still add to the cause by further improving on Cybersecurity index, national ethics framework and, data protection and privacy legislation.

Some of the indicators that have the potential to enhance a country's AI Readiness have been analysed from India's perspective along with latest Global Rankings of P5 Nations and India in these areas. These are detailed below.

5.2.1 Cyber Security: Global Cybersecurity Index 2020

The Global Cybersecurity Index (GCI) was first launched in 2015 by the **International Telecommunication Union (ITU)** to measure the commitment of 193 ITU Member states and the State of Palestine to Cybersecurity. The aim was to help them identify the areas where they could improve so as to take actions and raise awareness of cybersecurity state worldwide. In its fourth edition, the Index maps 82 questions on cybersecurity commitments worldwide across following five pillars:

- Legal Measures
- Technical Measures
- Organisational Measures
- Capacity Development Measures
- Co-operation Measures

The global cyber security score and rankings of P5 nations and India are as under:

Table 8: ITU Global Cybersecurity Index 2020 Ranking of P5 Nations and India

Country	*Score*	*Rank (2020)*	*Rank (2018)*	*Change in Rank*
1. USA	100	1	2	+1
2. UK	99.54	2	1	-1
3. Russia	98.06	5	26	+21
4. France	97.6	9	3	-6
5. India	97.5	10	47	+37
6. China	92.53	33	27	-6

India has drastically improved its ranking since the last Cybersecurity Index published in 2018. It is mainly attributed to its relative strength in at least three out of the five pillars considered: Legal, Cooperation and Capacity Development measures. Organisational Measures is the area where there is potential growth. Pushing back China in global ranking indicates that India has come a long way in the last two years. This AI Readiness indicator is well poised to push India further up in AI Readiness Index 2022 rankings next year.

5.2.2 Supercomputers: Top500 List (2022)

As per the 59th edition of Top500 list of supercomputers released on 01 June 2022, China leads the pack with 173 supercomputers in the first 500 list. USA has regained the top spot having the fastest supercomputer in the world, named 'Frontier', the first supercomputer to achieve the maximal performance in exascale (10^{18}) range (R_{max} = 1.102 exaFLOPS/sec). India has three supercomputers in the Top500 list, the fastest being PARAM Siddhi-AI with R_{max} as 4.619 petaFLOPS, the other two being Pratyush and Mihir, both in petaFLOPS category as well. India ranks 12th (sharing the rank with two other countries) in terms of number of supercomputers in top 500 list.

Based on the Top500 Supercomputer List 2022, the Global Rankings of P5 nations and India is as under:

Table 9: Supercomputer based Global Ranking 2022 of P5 Nations and India

	Country	*Supercomputer Count in Top500 (June 2022)*	*Global Rank*	*Remarks*
1.	China	173	1	
2.	USA	128	2	Has the world's fastest super computer 'Frontier'
3.	France	22	5	
4.	UK	12	7	
5.	Russia	07	8	
6.	India	03	12	Joint 12th rank with two other countries

The completion of Phase 3 of National Supercomputer Mission (NSM) by the end of year 2022 may take India into List of Top 10 nations in the Top500 List by June 2023.

5.2.3 Cloud Computing: Latest Global Rankings

The latest global cloud computing score sheet ranked 24 countries based on seven pillars that measure the countries' preparedness to support the growth of cloud computing. 80% of the global ICT market is accounted for by these 24 countries in turn, signalling the AI Readiness of these countries. The seven pillars or policy categories are: (i) data privacy, (ii) security, (iii) cybercrime, (iv) intellectual property rights, (v) standards and international harmonisation, (vi) promotion of free trade and (vii) ICT readiness and broadband deployment. Germany tops the list with a score of 84 out of 100. The rankings of the P5 Nations and India are as follows:

Table 10: Latest Global Cloud Computing Ranking of P5 Nations and India

	Country	*Score*	*Ranking*
1.	USA	82.0	3
2.	UK	81.8	4
3.	France	79.6	8
4.	India	48.4	20
5.	Russia	45.0	21
6.	China	43.7	22

India scores over both Russia and China to be placed above them in rankings. However, India performs poorly in ICT readiness and broadband deployment. Unless it improves both, it may further slide in rankings below both Russia and China. This may affect its AI Readiness too. Same goes for Russia and China on security and cybercrime.

5.3 USE OF AI IN MILITARY MODERNISATION OF P5 NATIONS AND INDIA

Among nine nuclear-armed states, Pakistan and North Korea seem to be presently out of competition on AI Readiness wherein Pakistan ranks a lowly 117th in the index of 160 nations while North Korea does not even qualify to be included, in the final index, owing to not having values for even 50% of indicators considered for ranking of a country. However, Israel ranks 20th on AI Readiness and is a force to reckon with, closely following top four P5 nations, USA, UK, France and China, and much ahead of Russia (38th) and India (51st) on the list. Israel has also claimed to have fought the first ever AI war in May 2021 against PIJ, making the conflict swift and short, indicating the dawn of 5GW era. However, within the purview of this research work, only P5 Nations and India have been considered for discussing their potential to adopt AI, seen as third offset strategy after its launch by DoD in November 2014, and the game changer in 5GW for National Security; in the nuclear deterrent architecture for military modernisation.

- ***United States of America***

The United States is the birthplace of Artificial Intelligence as the discipline was born at the Dartmouth College, New Hampshire in 1956. Its resurgence in the beginning of the previous decade has synergised the political leadership which has called for a national level effort to thwart China's ambitions to overthrow USA from its position of technical hegemony in the field of AI by 2030.

The United States is currently modernising its nuclear triad by either upgradation or replacement of its nuclear delivery systems. It is likely that AI and its subset Machine Learning will have a role to play in the modernisation programme, in areas such as force applications, battlespace awareness, force protection and logistics. The state of adoption of AI in the United States' nuclear deterrence architecture, with details of application areas, status of the projects and **confirmed AI use** is tabulated as under:

Table 11: Details of Projects with confirmed AI use (USA)

Application Area	*Status*	*AI Use Details*
Early Warning And Intelligence, Surveillance And Reconnaissance		
1. AI for data collection and analysis	R&D (Project Maven)	This makes use of machine learning so as to automatically analyse video surveillance footage that has been gathered during CI Operations.
2. ISR/remote sensing	R&D (Perdix UAV Swarm)	100 UAVs can be used to conduct collaborative ISR operations autonomously.
3. ISR/remote sensing	R&D (X-47B unmanned aerial vehicle)	Autonomous take-off and landing, navigation in non-communication areas environments and in-flight refuelling.
4. ISR/remote sensing	Production (Orca XLUUV)	Autonomous navigation capabilities.
Command and Control		
5. Decision support systems	R&D (Deep Green)	Has the ability to evaluate options, develop alternatives and evaluate the impact of the decision to assist commanders develop or generate courses of action.

Application Area	*Status*	*AI Use Details*
Precision Strike and Delivery		
6. Missile/Air/ Space Defence	Deployed (Aegis Ballistic Missile Defence Systems)	Makes use of an active radar seeker.
Other applications		
7. Cyber/Electronic Information Warfare	R&D (2016 DARPA Cyber Grand Challenge)	Autonomous detection and evaluation; Patch software vulnerabilities.
8. Physical Security	R&D (Sea Hunter autonomous vehicle.)	Autonomous detection, tracking and trailing of submarines.
9. Physical Security	R&D (Control Architecture for Robotic Agent and Command and Sensing or CARACAS)	Surface Vessels and UAVs given access to conduct area-denial manoeuvres autonomously.

Source: SIPRI

- ***Russia***

In September 2017, Russian President Vladimir Putin made a sweeping statement that, 'AI is the future, not only for Russia, but for all humankind.' While the focus of draft National Security issued in October 2019 is on civilian applications and military AI policy has been kept separate, the Russian government inspired by Putin's declaration consider AI as the game changer and Russia will need to harness its enormous potential for military use to maintain its hard power ambition. The areas of interest for AI use as analysed by Russian Military Experts include Battlefield and Force Management, Command, Control, Communication, Computers, Intelligence, Surveillance and Reconnaissance (C4ISR), remotely operated strike and reconnaissance, autonomous system, battlefield security & force protection and simulation & training. Russia has been critical of intergovernmental discussion on LAWS and believes that human supervision and control is not necessary to ensure responsible use of autonomous weapons. Russia seems to keep enough elbow space so as to determine the extent up to which responsible use of AI is permissible and acceptable.

However, focus having shifted from AI challenges it needs to tackle, to the ongoing conflict with Ukraine; Russia in all probability is likely to slip further on this account, making it difficult to compete with China or the USA. The state of adoption of AI in Russia's nuclear deterrence architecture, with details of application areas, status of the projects and confirmed AI use is tabulated as under:

Table 12: Details of Projects with confirmed AI use (Russia)

Application Area	*Status*	*AI Use Details*
Early Warning And Intelligence, Surveillance And Reconnaissance		
1. AI for data collection and analysis	Deployed (National Defence Operations Centre)	Useful for the purpose of collecting and organizing information.
2. Remote sensing	Deployed (Kasatka Avionics System for Aircraft, Helicopters and UAVs)	Automatic detection of submarines and surface, ground and air targets.
Command and Control		
3. Command and Control	Deployed ('Perimetr' automated reserve command and control system.)	For the purpose to launch a nuclear strike based on data obtained from sensors which indicate a nuclear attack.
Precision Strike and Delivery		
4. Air Launched	Deployed (Autonomous board guidance and control systems to facilitate hypersonic cruise missile)	Maintenance and on-board control for cruise missiles.
5. Sea Launched	R&D (Poseidon Nuclear Powered: Nuclear Capable UWV)	Autonomous Dual-Use Platform
6. Ground Launched	R&D (Burevestnik nuclear-powered, nuclear-capable cruise missile.)	It is a long-range system which has the capability to change its course to avoid ballistic missiles in the defence zone.
7. Missile/Air/Space Defence	R&D (Land-based early warning radar)	AI enabled radar which is a central part for the automated command and control of the Russian Aerospace forces.
Other applications		
8. Physical Security	Deployed (Nerekhta autonomous combat vehicle)	Has the capability to select and eliminate targets in a fully automated mode.

Source: SIPRI

- ***United Kingdom***

The historical background of AI has deep connection with the United Kingdom. The AI and ML pioneer Alan Turing and the father of Artificial Neural network and Deep Learning, Geoffrey Hinton were both born and educated in the UK. The 2018 AI Sector Deal, an Industrial Strategy signals UK's ambitions of becoming 'the Best in the World'. It stresses on building prosperous communities throughout the nation and has no mention of military AI. However, British MoD believes that the key is to effectively integrate humans and machines into war fighting systems. The areas of interest for military use of AI as viewed by the MoD are capability enhancement in cyber war, weapon systems, logistics and coverage of battlefield. The UK is also currently modernising its nuclear programme, prominent step in this direction being replacement of Vanguard-class submarines with the new Dreadnought Class, likely to be inducted in early 2030.

The state of adoption of AI in the United Kingdom's nuclear deterrence architecture, with details of application areas, status of the projects and confirmed AI use is tabulated as under:

Table 13: Details of Projects with confirmed AI use (UK)

Application Area	*Status*	*AI Use Details*
Early Warning And Intelligence, Surveillance And Reconnaissance		
1. AI for data collection and analysis	R&D (SAPIENT Programme: Sensing for Asset Protection using Integrated Electronic Network Technology)	Capability to autonomously process and select the ISR information.
2. Remote sensing	R&D (XLUUV Programme)	Requirement of autonomous navigation capabilities to some extent.
Precision Strike and Delivery		
3. Air Launched	Production (Brimstone Fire-and-Forget Missile)	Missile has a conventional payload which has the ability to autonomously find a predefined target in a predefined area.
4. Missile/Air/ Space Defence	Deployed (Sea Ceptor Air Defence System)	Makes use of an active radar seeker.

Application Area	*Status*	*AI Use Details*
Other Applications		
5. Cyber/Electronic Information Warfare	Deployed (Darktrace)	Commercial technology that can autonomously detect and accordingly respond to the cyberattack.
6. Physical Security	Deployed (C-Hunter semi-submersible auto-nomous surface vehicle)	Autonomous navigation capability is included.

Source: SIPRI

- ***France***

AI has emerged as the top priority for France since 2017. While strategy focusses on civilian use of AI, the Defence Ministry has drawn a 7-year plan (2019-2025) that sets the course for France's military investment. The strategic interest in AI continues for the country under the leadership of Emmanuel Macron, the French President, re-elected in April 2022. Ministry of the Armed Forces (MAF) have clarified of France's strategic autonomy in future. France does not entirely present the use of autonomous systems but views them as enhancers of the Armed Forces' efficiency, alleviating risks for the military personnel within ambit of international law. The priority areas identified by MAF for AI use are: i) Informed Decision Making, ii) ISR Collection and Analysis, iii) Collaborative Operations, iv) Robotics for dull, dirty and dangerous (3D) Tasks, v) Cyber warfare and vi) Logistics & Maintenance. France is also engaged in military modernisation, intending to replace its Triomphant-class submarines with an able successor such as SNLE-3G—a third-generation nuclear ballistic missile submarine around 2035 that could see the present century through.

The state of adoption of AI in French nuclear deterrence architecture, with details of application areas, status of the projects and confirmed AI use is tabulated as under:

Table 14: Details of Projects with confirmed AI use (France)

Application Area	*Status*	*AI Use Details*
Early Warning And Intelligence, Surveillance And Reconnaissance		
1. AI for data collection and analysis	R&D (Ongoing research as per MAF'S AI Strategy.)	Confirmed use of AI
2. Remote sensing	R&D (Thales: Stealthy Under-water and Surface Vehicle for long-lasting and long-distance operations.)	Confirmed use of AI
Command and Control		
3. Autonomous Wingman	R&D Man-machine teaming study	Can enable the command and control of autonomous unmanned wingman for a manned aircraft.
Precision Strike and Delivery		
4. Air Launched	R&D (Dassault: nEUROn Unmanned Combat Aerial Vehicle.)	Autonomous take-off and landing.
5. Missile/Air/Space Defence	Deployed (Artemis Infrared search and track system)	Automatic passive detection for up to 200 targets.
Other Applications		
6. Cyber/Electronic Information Warfare	R&D (Research ongoing according to MAF'S AI Strategy)	Autonomous detection and evaluation; Patch software vulnerabilities.

Source: SIPRI

- ***China***

The Chinese leadership under President Xi Jingping has already come out with the most comprehensive AI Strategy in 2017 and aspires to become world leaders in AI by 2030. The dual use of AI suits to China's push towards military-civil fusion. This suggests that the cross-over between civilian and military, as also the conventional and the nuclear domains is likely to proliferate.

China strongly believes that the military AI is critical to its future military aspirations. This is bolstered by the 2018 statement by the Director of the CMC's Science and Technology Commission, 'Facing

Disruptive Technology, we must seize the opportunity to change paradigms; if you don't disrupt, you'll be disrupted!' As regards autonomy and LAWS, Chinese AI Strategy documents do not give a clear picture, how Chinese intend to use or restrict military AI. They seem to legitimise the use of autonomous weapons with their narrow definition of LAWS as one having lethality, autonomy, impossibility of termination, indiscriminate effect and evolution capability so as to learn autonomously.

China invests massively in AI and R&D and has the world's largest AI decacorn in the industry named 'Byte Dance' worth $140 billion. As part of the Mega Innovation Plan, the Ministry of Science and Technology (MOST) announced 'AI 2.0' with emphasis on data intelligence, cross-media intelligence, swarm intelligence, hybrid-augmented intelligence and autonomous intelligent systems.

The state of adoption of AI in Chinese nuclear deterrence architecture, with details of application areas, status of the projects and confirmed AI use is tabulated as under:

Table 15: Details of Projects with confirmed AI use (China)

Application Area	*Status*	*AI Use Details*
Early Warning And Intelligence, Surveillance And Reconnaissance		
1. Data Collection & Analysis	R&D (Over-the-horizon OTH-B long-range radar)	Confirmed use of AI
Command and Control		
2. Battlefield Conditions and Management	Production (Joint Operations Command and Control Advanced Concepts Demonstration System.)	Based on the study of the US Program called 'Deep Green'
Precision Strike and Delivery		
3. Air Launched	Production (DF-ZF Hypersonic glide vehicle, currently mounted on DF-17 Solid-Fuelled, Road-Mobile, Short-Range Ballistic Missile.)	Machine Learning and Autonomy for guidance and manoeuvrability.

Application Area	*Status*	*AI Use Details*
4. Sea Launched	R&D (XLUUV, HSU-001)	Has the autonomous navigation capability.
Other Applications		
5. Cyber/Electronic Information Warfare	R&D (Work being done along the directives of the Chinese Government.)	Confirmed use of AI.
6. Physical Security	R&D (Work being done along the directives of the Chinese Government.)	Confirmed use of AI.

Source: SIPRI

- ***India***

India stepped into the AI field with convening of two task forces – one under MoCI to explore the use of AI to solve socio-economic problems of the citizens and the other under MoD to study the strategic implications of AI from national security perspective. Based on the recommendations from these two task forces, Indian apex think-tank NITI Aayog published the National Strategy for AI (NSAI) in June 2018. In the CCW Framework, India stresses on risks to strategic stability posed by the development of LAWS; an issue that merits greater consideration in the present scenario. Though CAIR, the dedicated DRDO AI Lab established in 1986, works on AI, robotics and intelligent control systems and primarily focusses on development of military applications of AI in India, the country has to improve its ability to collect, validate and standardise, correlate and archive relevant AI data as pointed by the MoCI taskforce led by Prof. V Kamakoti of IIT Madras. The infrastructure development, R&D efforts, foreign collaborations and interactions with the industry and academia need to be vigorously pursued to realise the AI potential, pegged at adding $1 trillion to the Indian Economy by 2035, as perceived by NITI Aayog.

India lags behind China and even Pakistan in the number of nuclear stockpile with a total of 160 nuclear warheads presently. China, presently having 350 nuclear stockpiles is estimated to top the '1000 Nuclear Warheads' by the end of the decade. However, China's ruling communist party has been warned by their top foreign policy advisor,

Jia Qingguo that the blind pursuit of "absolute national security" coupled with huge spending on defence can lead to economic collapse akin to the Soviet Union. Notwithstanding, India in need of a minimum nuclear stockpile to deter both adversaries, will need to keep the Buddha smiling and at the same time put plans in place to utilise AI for the purpose. However, its use in near future in the nuclear-deterrent architecture seems a remote possibility. Its role may most likely grow due to introduction of nuclear-capable 'Nirbhay', long range, subsonic cruise missile. The state of adoption of AI in Indian nuclear deterrence architecture, with details of application areas, status of the projects and confirmed AI use or otherwise is tabulated as under:

Table 16: Details of Projects with confirmed AI use (India)

Application Area	*Status*	*AI Use Details*
Early Warning And Intelligence, Surveillance And Reconnaissance		
1. Reconnaissance and Surveillance	R&D (**Tapas 201/Rustom-2** medium-altitude long-endurance (MALE) UAV	Confirmed use of AI.
2. Reconnaissance and Surveillance	R&D (**Adamya UAV**)	Autonomous Underwater Vehicle.
3. Reconnaissance and Surveillance	**Status not known** (**Netra UAV**)	Autonomous Navigation and Guidance System
4. Reconnaissance and Surveillance	R&D (Multi Agent Robotics Framework (MARF) System)	Robot collaboration for surveillance and reconnaissance facilitated by this system.
5. Reconnaissance and Surveillance	**Status not known** (**Himshakti** Integrated Electronic Warfare System)	Application of AI for surveillance, analysis, interception, finding direction and position fixing, signal intelligence and jamming all communications and radar signals.
Command and Control		
6. Information Retrieval, Processing and Storage	Command, Information and Decision Support System (**CIDSS**)	AI would be helpful in facilitating functions like: Storage, Retrieval, Processing (Filtering, Correlation and Fusion) along with Tactical Data Visualisation and providing an effective decision support system.

Application Area	*Status*	*AI Use Details*
Precision Strike and Delivery		
7. Air, Sea, Ground Launched	Production (**BrahMos** supersonic cruise missile/ land-attack cruise missile.)	AI use **not** confirmed.
8. Air, Sea, Ground Launched	R&D (**BrahMos-II**/NG Hypersonic Cruise Missile)	AI may enhance speed and manoeuvrability to help evade any kind of radar detection.
9. Ground Launched	Production (**Nirbhay Long-Range Subsonic Cruise Missile**)	May use AI for manoeuvrability for precision strikes.
Other applications		
10. Physical Security	R&D (UAVs to detect radiation and for disposal of IEDs)	AI use confirmed.

Source: SIPRI

To sum it up, the comparative study between India and the P5 nations suggests, India has made considerable growth in its vision and technology enhancement over last five years since it took its baby steps in the AI field in 2017. Her standings on the world stage in terms of key parameters vital for development of AI are convincing and indicate that next five years will set the stage for India to be a force to reckon with in AI arena. It is heartening to find that there is no lack of consistent support from the government as also the technological capability and talent. Only laws and regulations need to be tweaked to steer in the right direction. The infrastructure push is the only parameter that may be lacking, where right steps taken now can plug the voids in time to enable India make its presence felt on the AI front. This aspect is not worrying though, as the initiatives already taken will bear fruits in short-term, if monitored well. It is high time; India drastically improved its dismal ranking on Multi-dimensional Poverty Index (MPI), Global Hunger Index (GHI) and Human Development Index (HDI) too, in its pursuit of excellence in Artificial Intelligence field. Time will tell.

6

Roadmap: Important Strategies of Artificial Intelligence for National Security

6.1 CONCERNS RELATED TO THE USE OF AI

Autonomous systems with in-built AI are proving to be a boon to the military as they reduce the risk to soldiers and cut costs while replacing them in so-called dull, dirty or dangerous tasks. In essence, they have become a tactical and strategic requirement, as they tend to surprise the enemy with AI's capability to produce unconventional results thus providing an advantage in combat.

However, it is dangerously naive to think that the technology is neutral. The worst aspects of the human behaviour are fed to the machines to replicate. Humans encode their historical biases into the data, then entrust to AI such crucial functions as predictive policing and recommend criminal sentences. Some language processing programs develop gender bias. Thus, AI inherits the racism of its creators, rather than being a 'levelling force'. Conspiracy theories have become the most 'powerful narratives of our time'. Such biases if undetected and incorporated into the systems with lethal effects may have significant implications.

The AI-based LAWS have been the central focus as part of DOD's 'Third Offset Strategy' because they tend to give technological edge to the United States against its principal competitor China. The systems being autonomous, is mainly attributed to the 'algorithmic intelligence' that they possess, which might cross the limits set by 'Law of Armed Conflict (LOAC)' or 'International Humanitarian Law (IHL)'. There is a raging debate to ban LAWS, mainly triggered by the concerns shown by all stakeholders including technology experts, public and industry due to ethical, operational and strategic risk in use of AI-enabled systems.

In an interview with '**technology experts**' on **risks associated with use of AI** by the RAND Corporation, a research organisation conducting a study on ethical implications of military applications of AI as part of a project for US Air Force, the responses constituting top three factors forming the risks associated with the use of AI are as follows:

- Risks of vulnerabilities and dangerous errors (20%) to include spoofing or hacking, difficulty in differentiating between anomaly and threat, inability of AI to adapt to programming and incursion of dirty data (operational risk).
- Increased risks of war (14%) from possibility of increased escalation, too fast decisions, arms proliferation and reduction in cost of war (strategic risk).
- Risk of overconfidence in results (12%), with systems fielded prior to full safety testing and over reliance on data (operational risk).

Similarly, in the '**public attitude**' survey on **ethics of AI in war**, conducted by RAND Corporation wherein they framed a questionnaire of 26 questions related to ethical concerns, the public opinion or the answers by the respondents suggested that these following were the three factors that shared their opinion:

- General Ethics of AI: support for a ban on AWS.
- Scenarios demonstrating non-lethal autonomy: Swarm force Protection, Data Analysis for targeting, recommendations to commanders, sentry robots at check points, fighter jet with a return-to-base function.
- Scenarios that demonstrate unconstrained autonomy: Missiles that search and destroy without human authorisation,

generating fake videos (Deep fakes), fighter jet with a complete-mission function.

As far as ethical concerns shown by industry, private sector in particular is concerned some companies are refusing to collaborate with DOD due to government's use of AI in surveillance or weapons systems. Google cancelled government contracts for two acquired robotic companies and prohibited another acquired AI-software start-up 'DeepMind' from future government work. More significant is the withdrawal of Google, under pressure from its employees, from Project Maven, barely after a year of supporting DOD on building a customised AI engine to detect objects in imagery collected by drones, a humungous and time consuming task for humans. This happened despite Project Maven having image-recognition techniques involved, which by no means are "autonomous weapon systems". This shows the seriousness of the concern that has led to military experts being vocal on requirement of a more conservative approach to AI development by the USA, noting that it would be unethical to sacrifice safety standards for the sake of external time pressures from competitors like Russia and China.

Chinese intent of being the leader in AI by 2030 may result in comparatively less safe and more risk-accepting applications, as perceived by experts watching the single focus of China on weapon research. Similarly, Russia is already known to use AI technologies for information operations directed against its adversaries. Ironically, Ukraine is believed to be using 'controversial AI' technique to win digital war against Russia in the ongoing conflict between the two nations. They have been assisted by an AI firm 'Clearview' based in the United States of America, that uses facial recognition techniques to identify the Russian deceased soldiers from its two billion images in the repository, with an access to Russian social media. Clearview AI's powerful face search engine has helped Ukraine to disseminate information of these deceased Russian soldiers on social media to their mothers to collect their bodies. Hence, it is not Russia at the moment, but Ukraine that is using American AI firm to prosecute 'Information Warfare' against Russia. Whether this is staged by a silent nod from the USA, which is a sworn adversary of Russia, can be gauged from the location of the AI firm 'Clearview'. Notwithstanding above, there is rage over Clearview AI's privacy practices and personal privacy being eroded by the firm.

The existing UN Convention on 'Certain Conventional Weapons' (CCW) however, has made the sincerest effort and focus on banning or regulating the use of such systems. The discussion on LAWS formally began in 2014 and the last convention was held in 2021. During the CCW Convention of Group of Governmental Experts (GGE) in August 2021, though disagreement still existed, shape of necessary policy response now seems clear. Richard Moyes, the policy and strategy expert working on current focus areas such as LAWS, in his analysis states that LAWS must be understandable, reliable and limitable in space and time within the framework of human control, to be sufficiently predictable. However, the central structure was divided into two components—one seeking legal response and the other calling for political outcome. Countries like USA, UK, Russia and India rejected the legal response. Richard Moyes believes that against this background, a legal instrument is taking shape, one that responds to serious moral challenge that is of importance to the society.

Although LAWS may be a decade away, failure of GGE to issue an official guidance for development and use of LAWS even after seven years, made one observer to remark that the international community is in danger of 'the pace of diplomacy falling behind the speed of technological advancement.'

India's Perspective. India, just as vibrant a democracy as the United States of America, that she is, needs to play a proactive role to prioritise its own economic and national security. Taking a cue from China that has been very active in the international deliberations and participation in the standards-setting bodies to set standards on controversial aspects of AI, so as to ensure that their products are critical features of AI in future, India must be more active in agenda-setting platforms. Being the founding member of a strong Global Partnership on Artificial Intelligence (GPAI) alliance comprising 25 nations, hosted by Organisation for Economic Cooperation and Development (OECD), India should leverage this huge platform, backed by its National Strategy on AI that stresses on ethics, privacy and security towards responsible AI for all, to place its principles in all possible forums with initiatives on the development of ethical principles and standards. To ensure this, an inclusive global governance institutional architecture may be required.

6.2 FORMULATING AN AI ROADMAP: POTENTIAL CHALLENGES

While AI, being a dual technology and truly disruptive, has the tremendous potential to provide benefits to a wide range of sectors, adoption has mainly been driven from a commercial perspective. National Strategy for AI plays an important role in providing guidance towards large-scale adoption of AI for solving societal needs and at the same time facilitating the Indian Armed Forces to ensure national security by securing their very sensitive land and maritime borders, that extend to over 15000 kilometres shared with six nations and 7500 kilometres shared with seven nations respectively. As India has already taken its first step towards building AI vision, there is a requirement to prepare a roadmap of important AI strategies to set a clear and time-bound goal to achieve, supporting India's national security objectives and ensuring continued efficacy of the Indian Armed Forces and the highest echelons of Indian leadership.

Before the roadmap is charted, some potential challenges that have been identified and need to be considered so as to be addressed while the roadmap is drawn for important AI strategies are as under:

- Lack of a formal 'National Security Strategy'.
- Lack of Innovation and Research & Development culture.
- Enabling Data and Infrastructure Ecosystem.
- Developing Technology Ecosystem, Re-skilling and Training for future, developing AI Talent Pool, re-setting curricula in schools and re-engineering of courses in technical colleges and arresting brain-drain.
- Developing Bilateral and Multilateral Partnerships.
- Collaboration among various entities: academia, industry and research institutions.

- Regulatory mechanisms on Ethics, Privacy and Security associated with AI use.
- Earmarking of Budget for AI development and investment by DPSUs and Private Sector to tap potential business in AI.

6.3 SUGGESTED ROADMAP: IMPORTANT STRATEGIES OF AI FOR NATIONAL SECURITY

The suggested roadmap for important strategies of AI is intended to provide a guidance to achieve the national security objectives in a time-bound manner. As India has taken the plunge a little late, the suggested strategies will maximise the late-mover's advantage. Each recommendation is divided into several actions that need to be completed within suggested timelines. To have the duration broad-based, goals are divided into three time-frames based on inter-se priority and progress of related initiatives and missions:

- Short-Term Goal (2-3 years), i.e., latest by 2025.
- Mid-Term Goal (5-8 years), i.e., latest by 2030.
- Long-Term Goal (10-13 years), i.e., latest by 2035.

6.3.1 Formulation of a formal National Security Strategy (short-term)

A formal National Security Strategy that eludes India even after 75 years of independence needs to be formulated at the earliest to provide necessary guidance to the government as well as the Armed Forces to effectively tackle India's threats and challenges. The 'important strategies of Artificial Intelligence' must be dovetailed into this Security Strategy so as to give impetus to non-military applications of AI in the focus areas recommended by the NITI Aayog and by government machinery. The Indian Armed Forces will get clarity on the aspects they must focus on so as to draw a strategy for military applications of AI and translate that into problem definition statements. The DRDO, DPSUs and industry then collaborate to enable transition from technology development to testing, trials and production within stipulated time frame and available resources. The National Security Strategy and the AI Roadmap contained in the document is recommended to be reviewed every 3-5 years for any adjustments and amendments required in the prevailing geo-political scenario.

The AI Strategies play a crucial role in realising all the objectives that could possibly form part of the National Security Strategy as and when it gets released in the public domain. Hence, a comprehensive AI strategy setting clear goals with milestones as 2025, 2030 and 2035 must be the top priority for the DPC, set up by the GoI in April 2018 for the purpose.

6.3.2 Innovation and R&D (short-term/mid-term)

India needs to develop the collaborative culture for research and development. Though India has some top-notch government funded technical institutions such as IITs, IISc, IIITs, IISERs and NITs, they are required to be connected so as to enable the collaborative research by the best talent pool of India. The following initiatives by the government are recommended:

- Centre of Excellence for AI (COREs) is recommended to be established initially at IISc, top five IITs (Bombay, Delhi, Kanpur, Kharagpur and Madras) and top four rankings IIITs (Hyderabad, Guwahati, Bengaluru and Jabalpur), to focus on core AI research. It must be ensured that scientists and researchers are relieved from managing any administrative overheads to devote their precious time solely on research.
- International Centres for Transformational AI (ICTAIs) must be established to focus on creating AI based applications, and comprise both government and private sector representation, funded by public-private partnership. Model ICTAI has been set up at Bengaluru and similarly, others need to be raised close to top engineering institutions and large cities to attract the best talent.
- The development of 15 Technology Innovations Hubs (TIH), six Application Innovation Hubs (AIH) and four Technology Transformation Research Parks (TTRPs) planned as part of National Mission for Cyber Physical System (including AI, ML and IoT), approved by the Union Cabinet in 2019 with a total

outlay of ₹ 3660 Crores for a period of five years up to 2023-24. These will focus on all sectors identified by NITI Aayog for development of AI for National Security and are expected to cultivate an innovation culture by drawing best of the talent for the purpose.

- The maximum advantage of collaborative research will be leveraged by connecting all COREs and ICTAIs together through high-speed link to the National Knowledge Network (NKN).
- The R&D and innovation in AI will require all research institutions, academic institutions, academia, industry (private sector) and start-ups to collaborate and interact on a common platform in National Interest so as to collectively produce tangible results.

Armed Forces. All three services need to ensure jointness for realising their AI goals. Towards this end, respective Centres of Excellence need to exchange innovative ideas by being connected through high-speed data network through tri-services Project 'Network for Spectrum'. A joint AI centre with best talents and representatives from Army, Air Force and Navy should be formed, interact with industry, academia and DRDO and draw their support in realising the fructification of respective use cases. They need to imbibe each other's best practices through synergised effort and MoD needs to play the role at the helm with two of its agencies in place for the AI purpose—DAIC and DAIPA. Earmarking 25% of DRDO budget for private sector or industry is a remarkable step by the government as the domain knowledge of DRDO and innovative capability of industry will come together to produce timely results.

6.3.3 Enabling Data Ecosystem and Infrastructure for AI Readiness (short-term)

India is ranked 51st on the Global AI Index 2021, primarily because of poor data and infrastructure ecosystem. This particular segment where India is placed 114th out of 160 nations that have been ranked in Global AI Index 2021 by Oxford Insights, has not helped India's cause as it slipped from 40th in 2020 to 51st rank in 2021, due to other countries overtaking India in this segment.

Data Ecosystem. Data is one of the primary drivers of AI solutions. However, access to intelligent data is required to feed the AI models. Though India is home to second largest number of internet users after China (658 million, only second to China's 1000 million users in February 2022 as per statista.com), structured and clean data representing the population as a whole is the requirement. Though latest deep learning algorithms derive value from unstructured data, it is not always possible to extract value from raw, unstructured data that is not clean and annotated. As regards data representativeness, the gender gap in internet access and mobile access as also the socio-economic gap in internet usage needs to be bridged to score high on data ecosystem.

Infrastructure. India is woefully lagging behind in all types of infrastructure valuable for AI development, such as telecommunications, 5G proliferation, number of supercomputers, internet bandwidth, cloud computing platform, semiconductor chain etc. However, giant steps have been taken in these areas and budget sanctioned wherever required. Firstly, 5G infrastructure roll-out is on the anvil as over 72000 MHz of spectrum with 20 years validity will be part of an auction scheduled for 26 July 2022. Secondly, the common cloud computing platform AIRAWAT with a budget of ₹ 7000 Crores will be established by 2025 positively. Thirdly, a series of supercomputers with a cumulative computing power of 50-60 peta FLOPS as part of NSM with a budget of ₹ 4500 Crores will be in place by 2024 positively. Fourthly, the package of US$ 10 billion by the GoI for indigenous resilient semiconductor chain and prospective QUAD Alliance for nourishing the industry is planned. All these projects need to be accomplished in mission-mode within stipulated time-frame as envisaged to realise the goals.

Armed Forces. A cloud system akin to NIC's Megh Raj under Project 'Kranti' also known as "Network for Spectrum" (NFS) for tri-services communication network will be operationalised in full capacity with expanded data centres for cloud computing network by the end of year 2023 positively. Relevant operational and personnel data pertaining to

Indian Armed Forces once transformed into digital format, can be stored securely on this platform. The entire relevant data will be readily available to be used to train AI models and other AI use cases under implementation or in pipeline through various funding routes. The NFS Cloud will make available 'common operational picture' (COP) to facilitate collaborative planning and combined execution, assisting all services to achieve situational awareness thereby synergising the efforts.

6.3.4 Nurturing Technology Sector (mid-term)

India needs to nurture its technology sector on all fronts to come up on AI Readiness. India ticks a few boxes positively on the technology front such as research papers published in AI (ranking third behind USA and China), producing of graduates in STEM (2.6 million in 2016 which is second only to China). However, India ranks fifth as far as citable documents are concerned, marginally ahead of some countries with much smaller STEM graduates like Germany and France. Also, the whopping STEM population of India does not focus much on research and innovation. India's competence in core research in AI is also not encouraging, with only a handful of researchers doing intensive research in AI concentrated at IISc or IITs. This trend will have to be reversed with the recommendations to intensify R&D and innovation above, all core institutions connected to NKN on a high-speed link connected to pooled cloud platform, AIRAWAT, i.e., AI Research, Analytics and Knowledge Assimilation Platform when it comes up within specified timeline.

Re-skilling of IT Professionals and Employed Workforce. The number of technology unicorns, especially AI unicorns will have to be enhanced in near future. India is ranked 4th in hosting technology unicorns behind USA, China and UK. They need to move to the league of having decacorns and hectocorns, specifically focussed on AI, like China and USA have. There has been a 10-fold increase in start-up funding over five years from 2014 to 2019. The hand holding by government in terms of funding and ease of business in the same manner will go a long way in producing more unicorns out of these start-ups, as AI development in identified sectors gains momentum.

Further, India in quest of transforming various sectors identified by NITI Aayog through AI, need to build the right skilled talent in order to build a robust ecosystem. It is a matter of concern and the focus needs to shift to bridge the AI skill gap. India has no dearth of IT professionals who can be suitably skilled in AI by leading EdTech companies, such as 'Great Learning'- India's leading EdTech start-up, technologically capable and having an access to quality faculty and highly acclaimed mentors for imparting online professional courses related to AI. The Future Skills platform, an initiative by National Association of Software and Services Companies (NASSCOM) will play an important role in imparting requisite skills to the target employed workforce.

Re-engineering of courses in technical colleges and re-setting of curriculum across schools. There is a requirement of re-aligning branches offered in engineering colleges to increase number of seats in AI and ML, Data Science and Cybersecurity across all colleges in India at the cost of some branches not in vogue such as Civil and Mechanical streams. This will go a long way in developing AI Pool with advanced research in the field as a mid-term goal. Schools also need the curricular reset to promote early adoption of AI and associated technologies. Basic courses of AI at the secondary level will have to be incorporated in the National Curriculum Framework (NCF) by National Council for Education, Research and Training (NCERT).

Arresting Brain-Drain. The ominous trend of fresh technical graduates and post-graduates from India's top-notch institutions moving out to the countries where they can earn more money and work in better conditions is something which continues unabated and needs to be looked into in the right earnest. All government funded top technical institutes like IISc, IITs, NITs and IIITs provide world class infrastructure to the students gaining entry into them. When it is time to pay back to the nation, they leave the country for greener pastures abroad. They contribute to the quality research, innovations, patents filed and finally to the economy thus providing technological edge to the country they inhabit. The government now needs to act and arrest this selfish trend which is in vogue since long, taking a leaf out of the procedures and best practices Indian Armed forces follow. In the Indian Armed forces, an officer who attends a professional course for higher qualifications, generally of the duration of one year and above, cannot leave the services for a minimum set period so as to contribute to the organisation after attaining higher skills fully sponsored by the government. The same should apply to all students passing out from a government-funded premier institution like IIT and IIM. The infrastructure and the pay package also need to be looked into by the government and industry to make the job lucrative. This must be drawn into the AI strategies so as to develop and nourish a large AI talent pool.

6.3.5 Bilateral and Multilateral Partnerships (short-term)

India is in the nascent stage of building foundational R&D capability and hence it will take some time to deliver indigenous technology solutions in AI. Interdependencies and multilateral collaborations are thus a necessity in high-tech sector such as Artificial Intelligence. The research in these areas relies in extensive cross-border movements of technology, talent and intellectual property (IP). India needs to develop bilateral and multilateral partnerships with friendly foreign countries that are advanced and ahead in the field of AI.

US-India Cooperation. US-India initiative on AI aims to foster AI innovation by sharing ideas and experiences, identifying new avenues in R&D and bilateral cooperation. India must make it count as it has gone far ahead in strengthening ties with USA since Cold War era. Just as China benefitted from the United States of America during its superpower tussle with the erstwhile USSR, to grow as principal competitor of the United States today, India now has its opportunity to gain primarily in the AI field from the United States of America, that is now vying to contain China which aspires to edge past and dominate the AI era by 2030. That is also the estimated timeline when China is slated to overtake the United States as the largest economy in the world and India overtakes Japan to become the third largest economy behind China and USA. One cannot be assured of the same vibrancy in Indo-US relationship in such a scenario then, as history is testimony to it. Now is the time to make it count.

QUAD AI partnership. Another key area to focus on is multilateral collaboration among the four QUAD Members. All of them are among top 10 research-oriented countries having top class research publications and citations. Joint Research opportunities leveraging each country's AI-related research prowess can go a long way in growth of all four nations, particularly India that ranks below each of the other three members who have more AI investment activity with China than they do with one another. To minimise dependency on China, specifically Japan, India and Australia need to collaborate more on AI.

GPAI. India being the founding member of GPAI, must make an effort to have bilateral or multilateral cooperation on AI with the nations that are advanced in AI, such as Singapore, Canada and Nordic countries, among 25 members of GPAI. Self-reliance is self-defeating when India is a late entry into the AI bandwagon and cross-border cooperation for AI readiness is the viable way out.

6.3.6 Regulatory Mechanisms on Ethics, Privacy and Security associated with AI development (mid-term/long-term)

Ethical concerns on use of AI-based systems have raised the raging debate across nations demanding accountable and explainable AI. Data being the fuel of AI solutions, appropriate handling of data, ensuring privacy and security is paramount. Data colonisation by foreign technological giants needs to be stopped through data protection frameworks and regulatory mechanisms. A robust IP framework is required for India to ride AI innovation wave. Challenges faced by the government despite initiatives in strengthening IP regime need to be talked through IP facilitation centres and adequate trainings of IP granting authorities, and judiciaries. We need to be ready to manage data ethically. As regards use of AI-based LAWS, it is some distance away; however, India must remain active on all forums and be vocal on regulatory mechanisms, keeping in view, its own priorities in terms of national security.

6.3.7 Dedicated Budget Estimates for AI (short-term/mid-term/long-term)

A nation in pursuit of cutting-edge technology to ensure national security cannot view the expenditure as a burden on economy. However, budget and funding needs to be decided by realities on ground, not by preposterous or illogical comparisons. Blind pursuit of Absolute National Security coupled with huge spending on defence can lead to a nation's economic collapse, so said China's top foreign policy advisor, Jia Qingguo, very recently this year warning the ruling Communist Party leader Xi Jingping. Government needs to allocate budget to different ministries identified as stakeholders for various infrastructure enhancing projects as the foundation is being laid for actual AI programs to run, as short-term goal. Thereafter, dedicated budget may be allocated for development of AI as a mid-term goal.

Industries and DPSUs. Under Make-II, the industries and Defence PSUs are required to invest in R&D to tap potential business in AI. However, on the same lines as the United States of America and China, the Government of India needs to make it compulsory for Indian Tech Giants and conglomerates to make investments till a robust and self-reliant infrastructure comes up to steer AI development. It must be borne in mind that this infrastructure will also help India realise inter-related Sustainable Development Goals (SDGs) by 2030 (mid-term).

Armed Forces. Budget estimates need to be dovetailed into the 10-year ICDP (long-term) that is prepared by the HQ IDS in consultation with the Service HQs every five years, comprising two five-year plans. Translating this into appropriate problem definition statements for R&D establishment and industry to enable transition to production with given time and resources will help set the budget estimate. Also, 5-year Defence Capital Acquisition Plan (DCAP) will include acquisitions for the next five years (mid-term), based on prioritised operational requirements. Based on DCAP, a two-year roll-on acquisition plan (short-term) called Annual Acquisition Plan (AAP) is prepared. This will enable to set the cash outgo in each financial year.

6.4 CONCLUSION

India's economy took a hit in the last two years due to an ever-increasing challenge faced by COVID-19 pandemic and presently by the ongoing geo-political disturbances. However, the nation as expected is bouncing back and the economy being nursed back to health. As estimated by the International Monetary Fund (IMF) in 2022, India has pipped France and the United Kingdom to be the fifth largest economy in the world by nominal GDP, standing at US$ 3.75 trillion presently. This bodes well for the AI mission in terms of enhancement in funding for the R&D efforts and infrastructure.

However, NITI Aayog, the government Think-Tank on all core issues of the country seems to have its task cut out as it grapples with the dilemma of addressing conflicting tasks such as furnishing a baseline report on National Multi-Dimensional Poverty Index (MPI), released in September 2021, indicating MPI as 0.118 and at the same time, lay out guidelines and directions for National AI Strategy for National Security, a forte of developed nations, especially P5 Nations who are ranked much higher in MPI, GHI and HDI than India, hunger and poverty being non-issues for them but India, that presently ranks very low on all three indices globally (66th out of 109 countries, 101st out of 116 countries and 131st out of 189 countries respectively). It will be interesting to see how the apex think-tank handles these tasks to achieve the desired outcome.

Further the full-blown military conflict between Russia and Ukraine since 24 Feb 2022 with an end not yet in sight, something impossible to even imagine in the present era of short-swift conflicts and changing character of warfare, threatens World order. Likewise, Chinese recent forays into Taiwan indicate an ominous sign on similar lines as Russia, and may escalate further leading to an attempt to annex the island country. Such prevailing situations present a sure shot recipe to trigger a world war.

In light of the global turmoil when the East and the West are divided on the Ukraine-Russia conflict issue, and with a belligerent China next door, it is imperative that India carefully charts the roadmap for important AI strategies towards strengthening the National Security. AI has the potential to add US$ 1 trillion to Indian Economy by 2035, as assessed by NITI Aayog based on the sectors they have recommended to focus on for AI applications. Handling the AI era in a planned manner will eventually solve societal problems and implement AI use cases envisaged for military applications while boosting economic growth of the country in the long-term. 'Economic heft' is central to National Security as it not only provides revenue to bolster our defences but also provides 'strategic heft', making us a more attractive strategic partner for other strong nations. It is a fact that as an individual, we can only respect and have faith in our nation, if we have self-respect and faith in ourselves. So, every individual in life and every nation in this world must endeavour to stand on one's own feet. We can only choose either of the two—'seek sympathy and serve the strong' or 'seek capability and competence'. India, seeking the latter, is at the cusp of glory. We, as a nation, have to seize the opportunities offered through the disruptive technology called 'Artificial Intelligence', so as to realise our long-term goal of breaking into top three nations leading in AI by 2030, as we march ahead to be among the top three economic superpowers within identical timeline.

The AI principles we operationalise, the investments we make in R&D, the national security applications we implement, the institutions and organisations we restructure, the bilateral and multilateral partnerships we forge, and the most important of all, the AI talent pool we cultivate and nourish, will set our strategic course in AI for National Security.

(Appendix 'A' to Para 3.5.2 of Chapter 3)

RESTRUCTURED ORGANISATION OF INDIAN ARMY

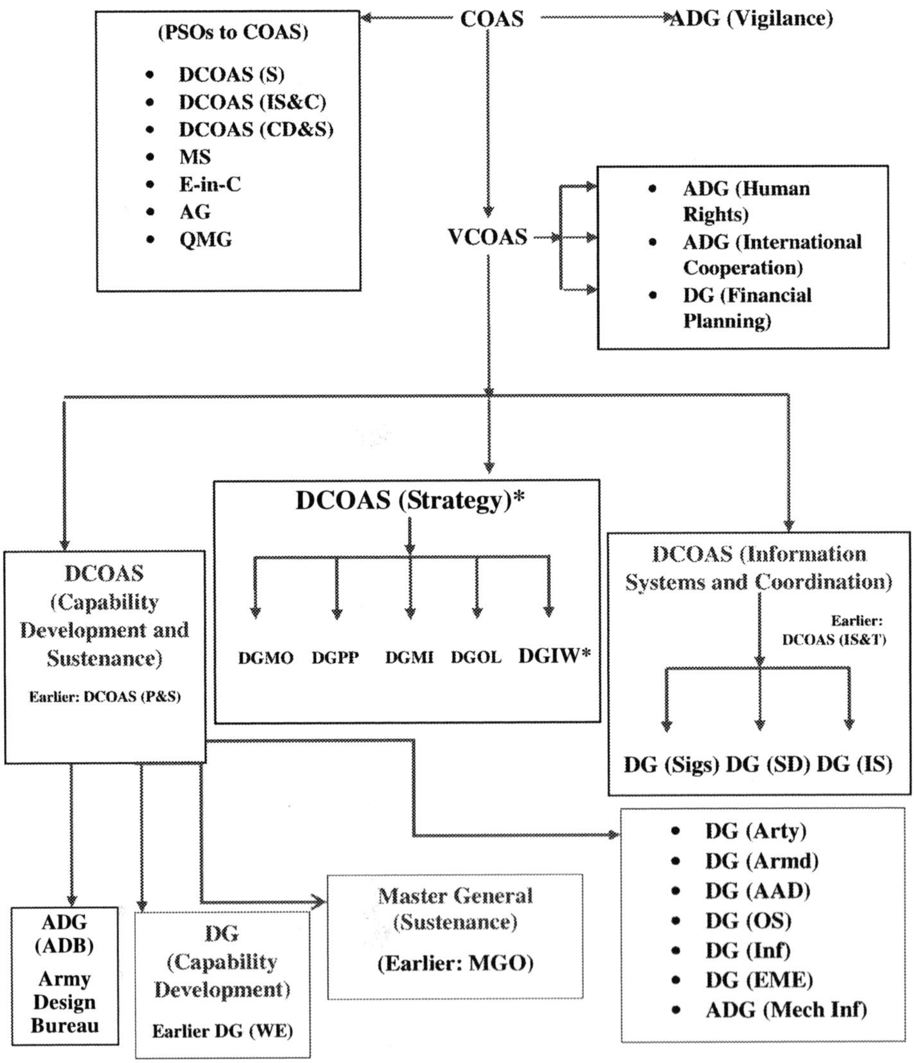

(Appendix 'B' to Para 4.1 of Chapter 4)

File No. 8(19)/2018-D (Coord/DDP)

GOVERNMENT OF INDIA
Ministry of Defence
Department of Defence Production

ORDER

South Block, New Delhi,
Dated: 08.02.2019

Subject: Implementation of the recommendations of the multi-stakeholder Task Force constituted by the Ministry of Defence for 'Strategic Implementation of Artificial Intelligence for National Security and Defence'.

Pursuant to the order of even no. dated 02.02.2018, the Task Force constituted by the Ministry of Defence for 'Strategic Implementation of Artificial Intelligence for National Security and Defence', has submitted its recommendations to the Ministry of Defence. Based on the recommendations, the following order is hereby issued:

2.1: Establish a High Level Defence AI Council (DAIC): DAIC shall be constituted with following members to provide necessary guidance to enable and effect development or tailoring of operating framework, policy level changes and structural support.

Hon'ble Raksha Mantri	Chairman
Chiefs of 3 Services	Member
Defence Secretary	Member
Secretary (DP)	Member Secretary
Secretary DRDO	Member
FA(DS)	Member
National Cyber Security Coordinator	Member CISC Member

Eminent representatives from industries and academia as members.

The following is a list of key responsibilities of DAIC:

- Enable Al adoption to be a part of defence strategy
- Provide strategic direction towards AI driven transformation in Defence
- Provide guidance and addressing issues related to data sharing
- Provide guidance in building strategic partnership with industry
- Review recommendations concerning acquisition of technology and startups
- Review the ethical, safe, secure and privacy assured usage of AI in defence
- Set policies in partnership with government institutions and industries to create deterrent for social and technology misuse.

The execution of above responsibilities and implementation of all recommendations may necessitate the development or tailoring of operating framework, policy level changes and structural support. The DAIC shall provide necessary guidance to enable and effect these changes.

DAIC shall convene twice a year. Additional meetings may be convened on need basis. The focus is to guide high quality and speedy adoption of Al-enabled systems at scale and to ensure that the issues and concerns raised to DAIC are duly addressed.

3. Integrate AI into India's Defence Strategy: All organizations in MoD recognize that Al is a "force multiplier' and shall thereby integrate and embed Al, in an appropriate manner, in their strategies. MoD Organizations for the purpose of this order would mean the three Services and the Coast Guard, IDS HQs, DoD DRDO, DDP and their attached offices including OFB and various DRDO labs, DGQA, DGAQA, DPSUs and other affiliated corporate entities.

4. Capacity Building within Defence: The cognitive-based decision making capability of a physical and computing system will go through significant change in years to come. Defence organisations need to have deep knowledge on contemporary research and development in these areas and need to contribute significantly in terms of research articles, data, patents, knowhow, trade secrets and licensing of these IPs. These deep pockets of knowledge have to be leveraged further in building current and future talent for defence needs.

4.1 AI training courses in all defence training centres and institutes: Application of Al in defence is pervasive. All defence training centres and academic institutions shall identify the need, prepare content, and offer AI related training and courses.

4.2 AI training of defence personnel: In order to develop a critical mass of data analysts, data scientists and AI specialists, MoD organizations, including Services shall be encouraged to introduce appropriately designed training modules in their in-service trainings. SHQs shall also assess their service requirements and identify right candidates and sponsor them for long-term courses leading to Diploma, Master and PhD degrees. Defence personnel should be encouraged to enrol in internships and sabbaticals at leading AI technology companies and academic institutes to rapidly gain AI capabilities.

5.1 Funding: Each SHQs shall earmark ₹ 100 crores for AI specific application development in each year for next 5 years from their annual budgetary allocations.

5.2 Budget: A budgetary allocation of ₹ 100 Crores made by MoD each year for next 5 years to Defence Al Project Agency (DAIPA) for implementation of recommendations given by Al Task Force including taking up AI projects, setting up AI related infrastructure, clearing & preparing Al related data, Capacity building, etc. in MoD Organisations.

5.3 The requirement of funds would be reviewed by DAIC from time to time and suitably fine-tuned.

6. Establish a Defence AI Project Agency (DAIPA): Formation of a Defence Al Project Agency (DAIPA) with Secretary (DP) as the ex officio head of the agency and members drawn from SHQs, IDS, DPSUs, DRDO, academia and industry partners.

Secretary (DP)	Chairman
AS (DP)	Member Secretary
3 Representatives of SHQs	Member
Representatives of IDS	Member
Representatives of DPSUs	Member
Representatives of DRDO	Member

Eminent representatives from industries and academia as members.

The DAIPA shall be responsible for taking all such steps as necessary for implementing this order. The key responsibilities of DAIPA will be to:

- Evolve and adopt a preferred technology stack within Defence establishments for development of Al Use Cases
- Evolve and adopt standards for technology development and delivery process for Al projects
- Review the categorisation and prioritisation of AI Use Cases at components, sub- system and system level including milestone-based fund allocation
- Tailor the standard operating procedures (SOPs) for the development and delivery of AI projects
- Formulate policy for IP Rights (IPR)
- Enable and review the on-time, on-budget, and high quality delivery of AI projects
- Review the scaling and adoption plan of Al-led and Al-enabled systems and processes with the user groups
- Incentivise the use of AI in existing systems and processes that demonstrate operating benefits
- Review the timely availability of talent in both user and technology development organisations
- Formulate policy for selection of, and contractual engagement with strategic industry partners

The DAIPA shall collaborate closely with SHQs, IDS HQs, DPSUs, DRDO, other MoD organisations, startups, technology development organisations, strategic to perform its roles and fulfil its responsibilities.

8/2/19
(R. C. Meena)
Deputy Secretary to Govt. of India
Tele: 2301 3705

All Members of the Committee Copy to:

(i) PS to RM,
(ii) NSA,
(iii) Chiefs of IN, IA, IAF,
(iv) Defence Secretary,
(v) Secretary, DRDO,
(vi) Secretary (DP),
(vii) Joint Secretary (P&C).

Bibliography

(Retd), Lt Gen Philip Campose. *" A National Security Strategy for India- The Way Forward", CLAWS Army No. 33098.* New Delhi: KW Publisher Pvt Ltd, 2018.

Aayog, NITI. *Approach Document for India: Part 1 - Principles for Responsible AI.* www.niti.gov.in, February 2021.

Aayog, NITI. *Approach Document for India: Part 2 - Operationalising Principles for Responsible AI.* www.niti.gov.in, August 2021.

Aayog, NITI. *Discussion Paper on National Strategy for AI.* www.niti.gov.in, June 2018.

AI and National Security. Congressional Research Service, November 2020.

Alliance, Business Software. *BSA Global Cloud Computing Scorecard.* BSA, 2020.

Army Design Bureau, Compendium Problem Definition Statements. Society of Indian Defence Manufacturers, 2020.

Behra, Laxman Kumar. *Bigger, not necessarily better: India's Defence Budget 2022-23, Issue No 523.* Observer Research Foundation, 23 February 2022.

Jadhav, Col. Ajinkya. *Leveraging Artificial Intelligence in the Indian Army, CLAWS Issue No 95.* CLAWS, 2021.

Kamokoti, V. *Report of the Artificial Intelligence Task Force.* www.niti.gov.in, February 2018.

Khare, Prof (Dr) Vijay. *" Influence of Social Media on India's Foreign Policy Making".* New Delhi: Pentagon Press, 2021.pp 21

Kumar, Amit. *National AI Policy Strategy of India and China: A Comparative Analysis.* ris.org.in, June 2021.

Lt Gen (Dr) RS Panwar, AVSM, SM, VSM (Retd). *"Artificial Intelligence in Military Operations: A Raging Debate, and Way Forward for the Indian Armed Forces".* New Delhi: Vij Books India Private Ltd., 2018.

Maj Gen Sanjay Bhide, YSM, VSM. *"International Security: A Psychologocial Approach".* New Delhi: Manas Publication, 2020.

others, Forrest E Morgan and. *'Military Applications of Artificial Intelligence' Ethical Concerns in an Uncertain World.* RAND Corporation, 2020.

others, Pablo Fuentes Nettel and. *Report on Government AI Readiness Index 2021.* Oxford Insights, 21st January 2022.

Rich, Elaine. *'Artificial Intelligence' Computer Science Series.* McGraw Hill Foundation, 1983.

Sinha, Brig Deepak. *Rebooting the Indian Army: A Doctrinal Approach to Force Restructuring.* Observer Research Foundation, February 2021.

Stephen De Spiegelaire, Matthijs Maas, Tim Suejis. *Artificial Intelligence and the Future of Defence.* The Hague Center for Strategic Studies, 2017.

Vincent Boulanin, Lora Saalman, Petr Topychkanov, Fei Su and Moa Peldan Carlson. *'Artificial Intelligence, Strategic Stability and Nuclear Risk.* Stockholm International Peace Research Institute (SIPRI), June 2020.

REFERENCES

Ahronheim, Anna. *Operation "Guardian of the Walls".* The Jerusalem Post, 27th May 2021.

AI and National Security. Congressional Research Service, November 2020.

Annis, Franklin. *'The Three Block War, Strategic Corporals and the Future Battlefield'.* Modern War Institute, 2nd March 2020.

Baru, Sanjaya. *'Abstain, but get stronger'.* Times of India, 28th February 2022.

Baru, Sanjaya. *'On Kyiv, sit on the fence'*. Times of India, 14th February 2022.

Baru, Sanjaya. *'Ride between East and West'*. Times of India, 28 April 2022.

Bhagat, Chetan. *'War as Reality TV'*. Times of India, 14th March 2022.

"CLAWS Issue Brief." February 2021.

Cowshish, Amit. "Distortions in the discourse on Modernisation of Armed Forces". *Journal of Defence Studies*, 2014.

Das, Manish Kumar Jha and Amit. "AI Technology in Military' will transform future warfare." *Business World*, August 2021.

Dasgupta, Probal. *'For Quad, Good News on China'*. Times of India, 25th May 2022.

Dhari, Amrendra Singh. "https://timesofindia.indiatimes.com/india/is-drdo-to-blame-for-indias-acute-import-dependence/articleshow/89952331.cms." 2022.

Eric Schmidt, Bob Work and others. *Final Report by National Security Commission on Artificial Intelligence.* NSCAI, October 2021.

Godbole, Amrut. *"Scale up national cloud for AI in Defence"*. Gateway House, 2020.

Goled, Shraddha. *"What are the scope and challenges of using AI in Military Operations."* November 2020.

Gurung, Shaurya Karanbir. *'Army Plans Cloud Storage for Operations Data'*. Economics Times, 2019.

Hoffman, James Mattis and Frank. "Future Warfare: The Rise of Hybrid Warfare". *CONNECTIONS (Consortium of Defence Academics and Security Studies Institute*, 2005.

Holmes, Kim R. *What is National Security?* The Heritage Foundation 2015 Index of US Military Strength, 2015.

Hooda, Lt. Gen. DS. *"India's National Security Strategy."* 2019.

"https://www.i-scoop.eu/convergence-ai-iot-big-data-analytics/." n.d.

Kelly, Kevin. *"The Three Breakthroughs That Have Finally Unleashed AI on the World.'* WIRED, October 27, 2014.

Kotasthane, Pranay. "https://timesofindia.indiatimes.com/blogs/voices/three-reasons-why-china's-tech-prowess-is-overhyped/." 2021.

Lonsdale, David J. *The Nature of War in the Information Age: Clauswitzian Future.* 2004.

MoD. *Defence Acquistion Procedure 2020.* mod.nic.in, 2020.

Panag, HS. *Decrease Military Pension, salary bill without reinventing wheel.* The Print, 17th February 2022.

Panagariya, Arvind. *'Time for Good Economics'.* Times of India, 12th March 2002.

Pati, Satavisa. *"Use of AI by Indian Army in the Borders ."* 20th October 2021.

Payne, Kenneth. *Artificial Intelligence: A Revolution in Strategic Affairs?* Rortledge T&F Online, 2018.

Saha, Ambuj. *Artificial Intelligence in Military Operations: Where does India Stand?* orfonline.org, August 2019.

Srivastava, Ajay. *"How India should ace the semiconductor game".* Times of India, 17th December 2021.

Stone, Peter. *"AI and Life in 2030 (100 Year Study on AI)."* 2016.

Subramaniam, AVM Arjun. "https://timesofindia.indiatimes.com/blogs/toi-edit-page/where-are-our-qiaos-and-wangs-ukraine-is-one-more-reminder-that-to-counter-china-india's-strategic-thinking-needs-a-massive-upgrade/." n.d., 2022.

Subramanian, L S. *Bharat Badal: 'Why Rural India needs a National Cloud Computing Platform.* Dataquest, April 2015.

Suri, Anirudh. *"China could use Russia's Cyber and Hybrid War playbook against India".* Times of India, 20th February 2022.

Sareen, Sushant. *"Between the lines: How the BJP and Congress manifestos hold up on National Security".* orfonline.org, 12th April 2019.

Varghese, Sangeeth. *'Is India upto China's Fifth Generation War?'.* The Hindu Business Line, 4th October 2020.

Websites:

https://mod.gov.in

https://www.drdo.org

https://www.niti.gov.in

https://www.drdo.org

https://indianarmy.nic.in

https://pib.gov.in

https://crsreports.congress.gov

https://www.gov.uk

https://www.defense.gov

https://www.indiaai.gov.in

https://www.oxfordinsights.com

https://www.sipri.org

https://www.rand.org

https://www.orfonline.org

https://www.coursera.org

https://www.wikipedia.org

https://www.analyticsindiamag.com

https://www.analyticsinsight.net

https://www.statista.com

https://tracxn.com

https://www.ibef.org

https://www.oecd.ai

https://iap.unido.org

https://www.spslandforces.com

Index